Build a Bridge and Get Over It!

By Paul Sheppard
With Rob Suggs

DEDICATION

This book is dedicated to:

my wife, Meredith
my daughter, Alicia
my son, Aaron
my mother, Peggy Sheppard
the memory of my father, Dr. Horace W. Sheppard Sr.
my siblings: Horace Jr., Pat, Gwen, and Kenny
the world's greatest church, Abundant Life Christian
Fellowship

Table of Contents

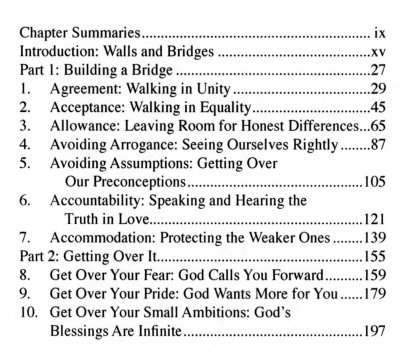

Chapter Summaries

Introduction: Walls and Bridges

Every day we discover a world increasingly driven by impatience, frustration, and outright anger. Can't we all just get along? Here we introduce the challenge of connecting with each other amidst the turmoil. And what does the book of Romans say to this theme? The stage is set.

Part 1: Building a Bridge

1. Agreement: Walking in Unity

Our first mistake is looking for uniformity in a world of diversity. What God wants is unity. We explore the differences between unison and harmony, and learn how we can turn contentious discord into beautiful music.

2. Acceptance: Walking in Equality

God accepted us in Christ—we didn't get to vote on that. Our goal, then, is to sharpen one another through our differences. But no one will listen to us until we earn the right to be heard; that happens through the power of caring. Parents, in particular, can learn to be more effective in their training by listening better. But does acceptance imply endorsement? The answer is observed through the story of Jesus and the woman caught in adultery. We need not condone or condemn. We explore practical examples from church life, and learn how the church can become "a soft place to fall."

3. Allowance: Leaving Room for Honest Differences

Now that we've accepted others, we need to recognize that there are issues on which we'll never agree. Therefore we make a point to allow for honest differences on certain issues. While there are essentials of the faith that cannot be compromised, there are also disputable issues with "wiggle room." Paul shows this principle in Romans. Here we learn how to walk in unity around the essentials while accepting our differences in the non-essentials. This chapter includes a light look at a few areas of dispute in our faith, and shows us how to find common ground at the Cross.

4. Avoiding Arrogance: Seeing Ourselves Rightly

What causes us to think we're better than others? We trust too much in our own traditions and interpretation. Paul said that neither party in a dispute has the right to be arrogant; both should give plenty of ground in the spirit of grace and humility. Ultimately, people answer to God, not us. So while making our own decisions, we must learn to respect those made by others as well. Otherwise we find ourselves drifting into hypocrisy because we tend to judge others on challenges and temptations we haven't faced. Again, we survey the "usual suspects" that bring out arrogance: opinions about appropriate clothing in today's church; smoking and drinking; and a confusing panorama of activities that Christians may or may not choose.

5. Avoiding Assumptions: Overcoming Our Preconceptions

We've all heard the popular rule of thumb, "What would Jesus Do?" Answering accurately is harder than we think. If the Bible doesn't clearly address a topic, how do we really know? Examples: worship styles; poverty vs. wealth. Too often we make many distinctions that God does not make. Jesus points the way toward a righteousness and unity that isn't based on human assumptions.

6. Accountability: Speaking and Hearing the Truth in Love

No matter how much we concentrate on unity and acceptance, the time will still come when we must confront a fellow believer. Does that mark a dead end for unity? Or is there a way to maintain love in the midst of significant disagreement? This chapter shows how to speak the truth in love and establish the atmosphere of a healthy debate, where listening is essential. We avoid two extremes: authoritarian control and flight in the avoidance of confrontation. We can learn to lovingly help others even when it's painful for both of us. Parenthood, again, provides a powerful forum for loving confrontation.

7. Accommodation: Protecting the Weaker Ones

The Apostle Paul speaks of avoiding some things simply because they are problems to the weaker brother or sister— stumbling blocks. Parents, for example, need to protect their children from exposure to certain issues, because their kids haven't reached the maturity required to handle these situations. We restrict our freedom in areas of contention voluntarily, out of love for others. In that way, we become "world class Christians," understanding the broad scope of God's reach and compassion for all people. Amusing examples from the past and present highlight this chapter, and we also look at the relationship between two contrasting temperaments, those of the disciples Peter and John.

Part 2: Getting Over It

In Part 1, we built a bridge together. We discovered the practical principles that forge connections to people who would normally challenge our patience. Now it's time to get over it! That means getting over ourselves, because we're going to be tested. Part 2 explores three basic areas that bring us to confront our own limitations. We find out how God lifts us beyond ourselves to breathtaking new potential and new joy as we become wiser and closer to our brothers and sisters in Christ.

8. Get Over Your Fear: God Calls You Forward

Cornelius and the Apostles were challenged to accept Paul—a known persecutor. Could they get over their fear? Opening ourselves to unity in the church and in our relationships can be scary. Change is always frightening and threatening, because we want to protect our turf. Just as the disciples conquered their fear and opened themselves to a more global Christianity, we must make way for what God is doing. We cannot be territorial, because what we give up is far less than the prize for which God exchanges it.

9. Get Over Your Pride: God Wants More for You

Peter had a pride issue, just as we so often do. His growth spiral focused on humility and letting God show him a new way to do things. Obedience to God takes us down a peg. Peter had to eat "unclean" food, then have fellowship with gentiles in a way that challenged all his life's training. We get into trouble when we confuse our view of the world with God's. In this chapter, the author recounts his own struggles with pride in learning to pastor a racially diverse church.

10. Get Over Your Small Ambitions: God's Blessings Are Infinite

Our final challenge is to accept the idea that God wants more for us than we want for ourselves. Are we ready to give up that comfort zone? Do we honestly want the life that comes with His blessings? If so, the result is an adventure that never ends. It begins with exposure to new wonders when we feel a holy discontent, a yearning for higher ground. Next there is enlightenment to new truths—about God and about ourselves, sometimes painfully. Finally, there is endorsement: we get the big picture of what God is doing. Then we become bridge-builders for life, crossing greater and greater canyons until we have reached the world for Christ, and become all that he intended for us to become.

Introduction

Walls and Bridges

⟿

I know exactly what happened to you just the other day. Remember? You were on your way across town, driving along and listening to music, your mind somewhere else entirely. Suddenly there was that ugly sound that startled you out of your reverie: a blaring horn. Another car pulled around you, and you saw the nasty glare as it passed. The driver was mouthing insults he knew you couldn't hear.

And what was your crime? Maybe you unknowingly blocked his restless lane-switching agenda. Could be that you pulled onto the road just one second before he came rocketing around the corner at jet speed. Maybe he's just the type who honks at everybody who dares to lurk between him and his destination.

Sure, I know it happened. I'm no prophet, and I haven't been spying on your life; I've simply described a scenario that happens nearly every week to nearly everyone who operates an automobile on nearly any street. Driving has become contentious, hasn't it? Something about the road brings out the worst in us all. We used to see a bumper sticker that read, "Honk if you love Jesus." I'd like to see one that says, "If you love Jesus . . . *stop honking!*"

Maybe you've noticed there's a lot of this thing going around: *anger*. And it's not just the usual "us versus them" brand of antagonism. It's not limited to the anonymous driver or the lady in the grocery store checkout line. Have you noticed how much we're also fighting among ourselves, up close and personal?

In too many marriages, we just can't get along.

Up and down the rows of workplace cubicles, we just can't get along.

On church committees, in condominium associations, and within extended families—nearly everywhere we go, we're choosing sides and drawing battle lines. Our generation has introduced cubicles to the office, gated communities to the neighborhood, and "personal vacations" to marriage. We just can't get along, so we build more and higher walls.

What is it about your life and mine? Is it the general stress level of the modern world? Is our killer pace wearing us down and placing that chip on our collective shoulder? Does it have something to do with the culture clashes that arise from living in a more diverse world? Have we simply forgotten the fine arts of cooperation, patience, and diplomacy?

This whole subject came up recently in my church. It wasn't a topic I set out to raise, but it leaped out of Scripture to confront us during Sunday worship. We were studying Paul's letter to the Romans together, and we'd reached the final two chapters of the book—chapters dealing squarely with the topic of getting along together. Very quickly I realized Paul, writing in the first century, had reached out through time to hit a nerve in the twenty-first century. Our people were eager for any level of guidance that might help them learn to live from day to day in a divisive, confrontational world.

As I preached these ancient, God-breathed words, I looked out on the faces in our sanctuary. I saw people of every race and every economic profile, because our church is a true microcosm of a diverse community. There were energetic teens, wise elders, and newcomers I'd yet to meet. But I saw a common story in their watchful eyes: daily struggles, clashing relationships, cross purposes; married couples who loved each other deeply but couldn't understand their conflicts; parents and children, working overtime to understand each other's minds; business folk who wondered if they could ever see eye to eye with their supervisors.

As the poet said, no man is an island complete unto himself. Sometimes the island sounds like a nice option, but the truth is that the world is one island in which we must coexist. Our peace of mind is dependent upon that skill our parents began teaching us in the nursery: playing well together, sharing our toys, making friends, and treating them as we would want to be treated. I remember Robert Fulghum's best-selling book from a few years back, *All I Really Need to Know I Learned in Kindergarten.* He had a point: it's all about the simple art of getting along together. But we can all agree that the world itself is much more challenging to navigate than a kindergarten classroom. There's a lot of kindergarten mentality on the highway, but without teachers on patrol.

I walk through the self-help section of the bookstore to find out what kinds of answers are available. There are a lot of titles about being assertive, getting one's own way, looking out for number one, and climbing over the competition to make it up the ladder of success. It seems as if the publishers are encouraging us to accept life as a war, and go for the kill. And we all know what happens with that mindset. We become even more focused on personal goals, we get even more entangled with other people who are doing the same, and we all end up miserable.

Maybe it's time to take another look at the wisdom of the ancients. It just could be that God's Word has a set of truths that could liberate us from the vicious cycles that make life so frustrating.

"I'm not so sure," I hear you say. "The Bible is fine, if you like stained glass words and high-toned sentiment. But Paul never drove on the Interstate. What does he know about the life in this new century? When he was alive, life was so simple."

I must disagree with you on that final point. Look just a bit closer at Paul's world, and I think you'll be surprised at the similarities to today's world.

The Moment of Decision

We want to know if there is wisdom from the ancients concerning this issue of getting along together. And we want to know whether that wisdom still works. Climb into a time machine with me, and we'll go find out for ourselves.

Let's set the dials for the birth of Christianity—the center point of history. I trust you know the basic facts of that. If our faith is true, then the Cross would represent the moment when our destiny was sealed. God became a man, lived in order that we would know how to live, and died that we need never die. Yet when he finally returned to heaven, he left behind a loose coalition made up of eleven unimpressive men. All of future Christianity depended upon these fishermen, tax collectors, and peasants.

This would have seemed to be no way to start a revolution if not for one factor: the entrance of the Spirit of God. He came into the world at the celebration known as Pentecost and made his home inside those very men. Electrified by the power and presence of the Holy Spirit, the disciples began to share the radical, exciting news about Jesus Christ.

So the first century might be the most exciting *time* to visit—but what about the *place*? Where else but Rome, the focus of history's greatest empire, at the height of its power.

Now you get the idea. We want to take a look at the most radical faith . . . at its most delicate moment . . . in its most dangerous setting.

Would you agree that this would make a suitable test for the validity of these ancient words of wisdom?

If you or I were trying to start the world's most powerful and dominant faith—an idea to drive history itself—Rome would be our last choice for setting up shop. The Roman Empire was a totalitarian regime that enforced its will through violence, and Rome was the eye of the hurricane. Revolutionary ideas were unwelcome.

Yet only two decades after the crucifixion of Jesus, a little church was brazenly forming itself in the very shadow of Caesar's throne. In the heart of Rome, believers dared to gather for the worship of a distant, obscure rabbi whom the Romans had nailed to a cross as a common criminal. In this city there would be cruel persecution. Peter and Paul, those two movers and shakers of the early church, would be executed here. Yet the blood of many martyrs would become seed for the blossoming of a faith that the world's most powerful empire could not hold back. In time, Christians would make this very city became their own capital. An empire based on might would be toppled by a faith based on submission.

It would take a miracle, of course. But it would also take unity. The adherents of this faith would have to stand together.

When in Rome

Imagine, then, that you're on your way to a worship service at the First Church of Rome. You're not heading for a towering steeple or an expensive family life center, of course. This is back in the day, so think house church. Expect a small, informal gathering and a simple time of singing, worship, encouragement, laughter, sharing the Lord's Supper, and reading a newly arrived letter from a favorite missionary friend.

As you make your way toward that gathering, you can't help but notice the pomp and pageantry all around you that is *Roma*. Slave auctions are here on this side of the street. Folks pass by going the other way, carrying sacrifices to the pagan gods. There are tough centurions exploiting their power, prostitutes plying their trades, city coins clinking, markets bustling, folks simply hanging out. This is the world's proudest city, and you can feel the pulse of power.

You think about where you're going, and suddenly you feel very insignificant. The church of Jesus Christ represents the way, the truth, and the life—you really believe that—but it is one tiny drop in a raging sea of paganism. Within three centuries, the very name of Jesus will topple this empire. But you're not privy to that information. If anyone told you that on this day in 56 A.D., you would laugh. A mouse would have a better chance in a stadium full of cats.

No, you're not thinking about toppling any empires. Merely surviving in such a city of such a world would be a nice start. Your brothers and sisters in Christ are good people. They love the Lord and they're excited about spreading the gospel. But even now there are tensions; folks just tend to see things through different lenses. This faction likes to have the singing first, then the Lord's Supper. This other faction likes to have the singing second. This other faction doesn't like singing at all. You realize that your group needs to be game-planning. It needs to be measuring strategies for hitting the streets and winning converts. But it's so easy for a fledgling church to become distracted, then divided, then dissolved.

That's why you're so eager to hear more from that new letter that's just arrived—the one from Paul, the missionary friend and mentor. You've already heard excerpts, and they're *amazing*—loaded with profound and exciting ideas about the meaning of life and faith. but Paul has saved one particular theme for last: *unity.* In storm-tossed times like these, everyone has to row together. The only way any ship ever crosses a sea is that everyone pulls the oars in the same direction. No divided church will make an impact in a pagan world; the bickering crew will vanish beneath the first wave.

Jesus, you've heard, put it this way: "Any kingdom divided against itself will be ruined, and a house divided against itself will fall" (Luke 11:17). He promised us power, but he prayed for us to have unity.

This letter to the Roman church, you feel, just might carry the keys to survival in this world, or a world in any time or place.

Letter Perfect

What motivated Paul to produce his lengthiest letter to this church? Our book of Romans has been placed first in order among all the letters of the New Testament. There is dominates our historic Christian faith, laying out the blue-print upon which we have built the church for two thousand years. If you happen to be explaining to a friend what it means to find salvation and follow Jesus, it is Romans whose verses you quote again and again.

Maybe the depth of this book represents the depth of Paul's heart for the city. At the time, visiting Rome was his dream. Yes, he was destined to be a prisoner and a martyr there. But for now, he was writing to believers he had never met. He needed to introduce himself and make a favor-able impression: "I planned many times to come to you," he explained, "but have been prevented from doing so until now" (Romans 1:13).

Paul, whose personal vision was to take the gospel to the gentiles (non-Jews), must have pictured the great city in his dreams. It boasted one million inhabitants, though a great many of them were slaves. He would have envisioned the legendary sites: the Forum, the Emperor's Palace, and the Circus Maximus.

In such a city of wonders, surely Christ would build a wonderful church. It would be a church that needed courage. It clearly lacked apostolic leadership, so far from Jerusalem, where the followers of Jesus made their base. The Jewish followers of Christ understood the foundation of their faith in Abraham, Moses, and the prophets; many of the Romans had never heard the stories. Therefore he wanted to paint for them the big picture of God's providential plan as it evolved through history and culminated in Christ. The book of Romans shows us that awesome canvas.

Paul begins his letter in a place that every reader can recognize: the human heart. In the first chapter, he talks about the sheer wickedness of humanity. Eventually such rebellion must come before the judgment of a holy God. Yet from the beginning the writer makes clear our hope, "the power of God for the salvation of everyone who believes" (Romans 1:16).

Paul goes on to carefully explain why any righteous action on our part is bound to fall short of the perfect standards of the Lord. We can't hope to please God even at our best, and therefore we stand condemned, deserving of eternal punishment. Yet through God's provision, his own perfect Son—the only worthy sacrifice—dies in our place. The apostle touches on the mysteries of God's great will as it moves through time, and how the Lord uses all things for our good and for the fulfillment of his purposes. (Romans 8)

Then, having shown the grand view of sin and salvation, Paul turns his attention to how we live together as a community of believers. The physical body of Christ departed for heaven, but we become the spiritual body of Christ. Each of us is an essential part of that body, through the various gifts he gave us. In Christ's church, we unite with our love and our gifts to form something vastly greater than the sum of its parts. We use our gifts and meet the needs of one another. Paul writes, "So in Christ we who are many form one body, and each member belongs to all the others" (Romans 12:5).

Now the apostle is bringing his amazing letter to its fitting conclusion. In Paul's words, "Each member belongs to all the others."

That is, all for one and one for all.

United We (Under)stand

There we have it: the wisdom of the ancients applied to the crisis of the moderns.

Think about what has already been proven. The issue is unity, and think about the church that received this teaching.

First, its members were not extraordinary. There's no reason to believe they were any more impressive than those eleven hapless disciples that Jesus left behind.

Second, the members were not uniform. Unity is easier when everyone looks alike, sounds alike, and acts alike. But Rome was an international city. This church would have been comprised of Jews and gentiles, Europeans and Asians, and even some from the northern shores of Africa. What in the world did they all have in common apart from a love of Christ? How could they walk in agreement? How could they survive the resistance of a pagan world?

For that matter, how did the disciples do it? The answer is to be found only in the awesome Spirit of God—the Spirit who bonds us together as that body of Christ that Paul described; the Spirit that works slowly but surely within us, to mold us to the image of Christ himself; the Spirit who gives us love for our brothers and sisters just when we desperately need it, who gives us the right words at precisely the right moment, who heals the rift that seemed irreparable.

Listen to two promises Jesus left for us: "Again, I tell you that if two of you on earth agree about anything you ask for, it will be done for you by my Father in heaven. For where two or three come together in my name, there am I with them" (Matthew 18:19-20).

Those words ring clear. They tell us that:
- Being together is sharing the presence of God.
- Agreeing together is sharing the power of God.

If I clearly understand what Jesus is saying, then this idea of unity is outrageously significant—perhaps the missing link in our faith today. To the extent that we can stay together, then we will feel his awesome presence among us. And to the extent that we can walk in agreement, we can walk through any door. There are no barriers, no limits.

What would happen if we ever became serious about unity? How would the church be transformed, and in what new light would the world begin to regard it?

What about your own life? Think about the key relationships in your life—in marriage, in family, in work, in friendship and community. There are so many high and thick walls that separate us both from fellow believers and those outside of the faith: walls of generational insensitivity, of denominational self-righteousness, of racial, socio-economic, or educational arrogance. Imagine those walls toppling to the ground, and the bricks coming together again to form *bridges*.

In the wonderful Word of God that we call the Bible, we find architectural plans for building those bridges. Let's be clear—this fallen and wayward world will never become one massive group hug. We will never see eye to eye with every single human being who crosses our path. Nor should we. But we *can* identify and tear down the walls that prevent us from practicing unity in the church and sharing the life and love of Christ with our not-yet-believing neighbors. And in so doing, we will discover how much better life can be when love begins to take the place of distrust, and when unity — not uniformity — begins to change believers from isolated guerilla warriors to a massive, tight, and disciplined army.

This book is about rediscovering that miraculous power that filled the disciples of the first century, against inconceivable odds. That power protected a fragile church in the world's most dangerous locale. It did more than protect — it raised the church to eventual dominance with a message of love and sacrifice rather than might and tyranny; of all things, a message from a Jewish peasant in an obscure province, who was put to death on a cross and who challenged the world, "Take up your cross and follow me."

That cross, as we all know, is a bridge between heaven and earth, uniting a perfect God with his suffering children. But it's also a bridge to connect people. That cross is powerful enough to knock down every wall that we have built between us. I hope you've brought your own challenges, your own battles and conflicts to this book. Whatever your greatest barrier may be — you have the chance to build a bridge and get over it.

Part 1:

Building a Bridge

1.

Agreement: Walking in Unity

L et me tell you about David Barrett.

He was a British airplane designer as a young man in the 1950s. The World War was over, but the Cold War was at its height. Barrett's supervisors wanted him to begin concentrating on missiles and warheads.

The only problem was that the young designer wasn't certain he wanted to do that with his life. He had actually been thinking seriously about a radical career change: the priesthood. Something had been happening inside Barrett since his university days at Cambridge. He had entered the school as a non-Christian heading for a career in science. One night he sat up suddenly in bed, awakened from a sound sleep. The non-believer was unaccountably certain that Christ was present in the room with him. Barrett felt a clear message, almost as if it had been spoken aloud: "Go to the ends of the earth."

As vivid as the experience was, Barrett stayed focused on the scientific life until 1952. It took the war department's reassignment to force his final decision. His life would be all about sending something to the ends of the earth. Would it be missiles or a message? The message won out.

The question was how could a priest use his scientific gifts and training? David Barrett had no intention of discarding them, because he knew God had made him as he was for a reason. In Kenya, he found his answer. The assignment there was to study the confusing network of East African tribal religions. This raised a question he found compelling. What about the world itself? How many distinct Christian groupings could be counted across the face of the globe? Had anyone ever attempted it? The physics of jet propulsion was kindergarten stuff next to this challenge!

David Barrett had his life's work. He spent four decades simply trying to catalogue the world's massive cluster of religious groupings, particularly those within Christianity. In 2001, at the age of 73, he released the second edition of his massive report, the 1,699-page World Christian Encyclopedia, published by Oxford University Press. Through 238 nations, he followed the growth and decline of various beliefs, and his numbers were staggering.

By 1985, when he moved his operations from Kenya to Richmond, Virginia, he had counted 20,000 Christian denominations. By 2001, he reckoned that there were 33,930 of them, and the momentum was only increasing.

Some observers actually felt that his numbers were conservative. Who could really be sure? David Barrett and his helpers tallied their count for nearly half a century, and their conclusion has been that five new Christian denominations are formed *every week*.

Now that we've tried to wrap our minds around *that*, let's rewind the tape about two thousand years. We'll join the evangelist named Paul, another man who wanted to go to the ends of the earth (God raises them up all the time).

We lean over Paul's shoulder to read these words he has penned to the church at Ephesus:

Make every effort to keep the unity of the Spirit through the bond of peace. There is one body and one Spirit— just as you were called to one hope when you were called—one Lord, one faith, one baptism; one God and Father of all, who is over all and through all and in all.

Ephesians 4:3-6, New International Version

The Power of One

Did you notice Paul's favorite word in that paragraph? I'll give you a hint: it's a number, and it's a good bit smaller than 33,000.

Six times Paul takes inventory of the basic elements of our faith, and each time he comes to a total of *one*. The first item he mentions is the church—the body of Christ—and there is only one. It is guided by the one Holy Spirit, and we live in the joy of one hope, through our one and only Father in heaven. The very foundation of our belief system is, "Hear, O Israel: The Lord our God, the Lord is one. Love the Lord your God with all your heart and with all your soul and with all your strength" (Deuteronomy 6:4-5). Translation: One God in our heaven, one love in our heart.

Paul shows how we should be transformed by that formula. Consider his words in the Ephesians passage: *One. Unity. The bond of peace.* Now think about the church of today.

Why is it so difficult for us to cling together and remain as that one tight family that we are so clearly called to be? What force inevitably tears apart the beauty of Christian fellowship? The watching world is not impressed. It sees war where there should be oneness.

David Barrett assumed he was leaving the business of battle when he entered the ministry. What he discovered was that every day, some church is coming apart at the seams over some new, molten disagreement. Every week, some new skirmish breaks out among the troops, Christians fighting themselves rather than the devil. Why, the devil might as well take a vacation. He doesn't need to do much work to keep the church from being what God meant it to be, because most of the time we foul it all up ourselves. As the comic strip character Pogo once said, "We have met the enemy . . . and he is us."

Imagine for a moment a world where Christians didn't major on disagreements. What would happen if we called off the internal wars and came together to bless the world as Christ intended? What if next year's survey showed fewer denominations than this year, because churches began forgiving, reconciling, and working together?

That's the church that Jesus intended—his eternal body of believers, bonded together in love and moving through the centuries, healing the sick, feeding the hungry, showing the hope and joy of eternal life to everyone on this planet.

Jesus wanted a better life for us, but he could see into the future. He knew what we would be up against. In the Upper Room, Christ prayed to the Father on behalf of you and me: "Protect them by the power of your name—the name you gave me—so that they may be one as we are one" (John 17:11). He spent these final moments with his friends, on the eve of his execution, talking about the deep unity of Father, Son, and Holy Ghost, which could empower the same unity among God's children.

We have the message that is the most important news the world has ever received. It is wonderful beyond imagining. With such an awesome and wondrous gospel to share, the question is inescapable:

Can't we all just get along?

It's not just a church issue, but one that impacts every relationship we have. Can we afford to have a little more harmony in our homes? Would the office be a better place to spend eight hours every day if we could all get along? You bet. We need to learn to walk in agreement. That's not a very controversial statement, for who is opposed to walking in agreement?

Nobody. Everyone wants to go along and get along. The problem is that we *do* have significant differences, and we can't pretend they're not there. It's simple hypocrisy to gloss over the fact that I'm a man and you're a woman, or that I'm black, and you're white, or that I'm from California and you're from Carolina. So let's begin with honesty, including honesty about God. Why refuse to see what is different about us? That's the best part of God's plan, and I'll explain how.

Unison and Harmony

Do you like music? Me too. If you look in the hymnal or listen to your song leader, you'll come across this term: *unison.* It has the same root word as unity or unify, which is the meaning of oneness. But the meaning is oneness of melody line; oneness of the notes we sing. If you and I sing, "Row, Row, Row Your Boat" together in unison, we sing identical notes at the same pitch, in the same octave (hopefully, that is—I haven't checked out your singing voice!). We sing together, but we sing exactly the same thing.

You know where this is going. That fact is that rather than singing in unison, we can sing in *harmony,* which means our notes are *intelligently different.* This doesn't mean I'm singing, "Row, Row, Row," while you sing, "Don't Rock the Boat, Baby." No, we need to be singing the same song, but in melodic lines that intentionally *complement* each other. Anyone listening to us hears one song, not two. But it sounds sweeter because we're singing in harmony—not in unison, not in jarring discord.

I love playing keyboards. In fact, I started playing the organ for my church's gospel choir when I was in my teens. I can sit at a piano and play you a simple melody, and you might applaud (just to be polite) at the end. But if I bring in rich, harmonious chords, you'll say, "That was *anointed!* Praise God!" I hope indeed that God anointed it, but the actual reason the chords sound so much better was the simple principle of harmony. When any of us are seen functioning in this world *tightly, as a team,* whether in business or marriage or anything else, the world may very well say, "That's impressive! I want to experience that."

Harmony is how we make beautiful music together, not only in song but also in life itself. Harmony doesn't require sameness. As a matter of fact, it requires a certain amount of difference. However, two parts share a goal, and they lock together to help each other reach that goal. We don't give up our individuality, but we contribute it like separate pieces of the puzzle, instruments in the orchestra, or parts of a high-performance automobile engine. We say, "I don't need to be another version of you to work with you. As a matter of fact, you and I together make we, and the total is far more powerful than you or me separately."

Michael Jordan played for the Chicago Bulls for several years before the team won a championship. It became a dynasty only when the five players suddenly learned to play with joy, based on the strengths and weaknesses of each starter. Center, guards, and forwards locked into perfect coordination and became something greater than the sum of five individual athletes. They became a machine that no team in the NBA could handle for a good bit of a decade.

The same principle is found everywhere—it's just the way God designed things. Differences are bridges, not walls. God intended them to pull us together rather than tear us apart. It's true of every point where two or more lives intersect with a common purpose.

Let's take marriage as an example. Have you ever seen a marriage that really and truly works, where there is outstanding harmony between husband and wife? Let me ask you whether it happened because the two of them were exactly alike. No, of course not. It's not about uniformity but complementary personalities and shared goals. Yet in too many marriages, one partner is bent on trying to make the other conform to his or her personality quirks. It's like trying to make a bolt become a nut—it flies in the face of the original design.

We were made as we are for God's purposes. One of the Bible verses that most shapes my ministry is, "We are God's workmanship, created in Christ Jesus to do good works, which God prepared in advance for us to do" (Ephesians 2:10). The words "prepared in advance" mean that we are not randomly put together, but intentionally designed for special tasks. Marriage is one of God's central deployments for fulfilling those tasks. Wouldn't you and your spouse rather make beautiful music together, in tight and melodious harmony, rather than the dull dirge of unison? It comes about when we embrace our differences and learn to make the most of them.

"Well," you say, "that sounds fine in principle. Next time we're out in the world doing those good works that God prepared in advance for us to do, we'll keep that in mind. But for the time being, we can't even agree on the thermostat. I like it five degrees cooler than my spouse. Unfortunately, we have to set the temperature in unison (one setting) if we're going to stay in the same room. So how do we sing *that* tune?"

First, give up on the goal of making your spouse agree with you on what temperature is comfortable. It's simply not going to happen.

Second, realize that being different is a *good* thing—even in the case of thermostats. It's simply a reminder that you are two different people, and therefore you have so much more to offer each other than if you were mirror images of one another.

Third, you already know how to find that harmony. You can do so through mutual understanding and patience, through compromise, through gentle negotiation. Find a place of agreement. Perhaps you can manage 2.5 degrees north of the ideal and your spouse can handle 2.5 degrees south. Perhaps you own the thermostat today, your spouse owns it tomorrow.

Love will find a way, and moreover, love just naturally gives more often than it takes. It finds that it really isn't interested in pushing forward to demand its rights. Love doesn't say, "You owe me." It says, "You know what? I don't care so much about the temperature as I do about seeing you happy. That's what gives me a warm feeling that is cool! Why don't you set the temp anywhere you want?"

Paul says, "Be devoted to one another in brotherly love. Honor one another above yourselves" (Romans 12:10). As Eugene Peterson's paraphrase *The Message* puts it, "Be good friends who love deeply; practice playing second fiddle."

And here's the best part about that: Any singer will tell you what happens at that moment when you lock in to perfect harmony. You don't think, "This sure is a lot of work." No, you believe you're in heaven for a moment. You want that feeling to go on forever. In music and in marriage, you really begin to receive at the moment you begin to give.

Why Opposites Attract

If only it didn't take so much experience to make that discovery of joyful harmony; if only we could see, from the beginning, the beauty of God's plan. If only we could experience life together in the full, multipart harmony that the great Choral Director planned for every one of us all along.

Instead, we make the sad mistake of thinking our own passions and preferences are the "right" ones, and forcing them on others. It doesn't have to be the color of my skin—it could be the color of the church carpet. It could be the plans for the church budget. It could be the kind of music that should be chosen, or how I read this Scripture compared to how you read it. It could even be my favorite football team. How exciting would sports be if there were only one team?

For some reason, we think the world will work better if we walk in lock step rather than simply walking in agreement. And from that point on, our prejudices polarize us.

Yet deep down you and I understand that we need each other. I know this is true because I observe the life mates that most people choose. Have you ever noticed that, when it comes time to get married, we tend to select someone very different from us? Sure, there are times when extrovert marries extrovert, or two quiet librarians end up together. But more often, opposites attract. I think it's because we instinctively understand that we need someone who fills in our blanks, and for whom we can do the same. Besides, we know ourselves well, and the last person we want to spend the rest of our lives with is someone exactly like us!

My parents fit that pattern. My dad was the classic *sanguine* personality, high in energy, always chattering and working the room. Mom, on the other hand, is the *phleg-matic* profile. She is a little introverted, always chilling out and laying low. When we had guests, they might take one of us aside and say, "Is anything wrong with your mother?" We would answer that no, actually this was a pretty good day for her! She just didn't express her emotion as readily as Dad.

It worked well that way. My parents were two gears who interlocked perfectly—two distinct notes in harmony. All of us have mental, emotional, spiritual, and physical components to our personalities, but the mix is a little different for each. With my mix or with yours, the result creates strengths and weaknesses. I'm a little more like my father, though not quite as much of a talker and people-person as he was. But I wouldn't get as far without my wife who is much better with the quiet details and logistics of life.

Disciples and Discord

Harmony, then, is the secret. Let's look at how it works in the spiritual realm. Acts 15, an account of Paul's travels, gives us a pretty good clue.

What was Paul's temperament? Anyone who has read much of the New Testament knows that he was the *choleric* type: the aggressive, take-charge leader. The cholerics in your life can be a little insistent at times. They're exactly the ones you want to follow on a battlefield, or some place where decisiveness is the name of the game. Not surprisingly, these folks can really rock the boat and make quick enemies—but they'll get that boat where it needs to go.

Paul was just the choleric that God needed for the wild setting of the first century. He led the charge into a world of darkness with a style that said, "Here's the way it's going to be—follow me!"

In Acts 15, for example, he was eager to get going on his second missionary journey. Barnabas, his right hand man, was up for the trip. It was his idea to bring along a young friend named John Mark.

The moment Barnabas mentioned that name, Paul's face changed. The glimmer left his eye and he said the equivalent of, "John Mark? Are you out of your mind, Barney? Not on my boat! This expedition is for grownup evangelists only."

You see, the young man in question had signed up for the last trip, and things hadn't worked out. John Mark had failed to weather the first crisis that had arisen. He had walked out halfway through the trip—and Paul had a long memory. As he saw it, this was the work of Christ we were talking about.

It was dead serious. There had been adversity before, and make no mistake, there was bound to be more of the same. Lives were on the line, and who wanted to crawl into the trenches with a proven deserter? Paul wanted to vote John Mark off the island.

Do you think the apostle was a little harsh? Remember his personality type and the tough task to which is applied. Paul was courageous, inspired, and visionary. But there was another point of view, and it was available from a man like Barnabas, a *melancholic* temperament.

Barnabas wasn't as flashy as the Apostle. He didn't write any books in our New Testament. Yet he had the sensitive touch when it came to people. He was compassionate, motivational, and redemptive. Where Paul saw failure, Barnabas saw potential; he saw in John Mark the young man who would be the first to write an account of the life of our Lord.

A person with the temperament of Barnabas might stand quietly in the shadows much of the time, but he'll step into the spotlight and take a stand when he feels the cause is significant. That's what the encourager Barnabas did in this situation. He was John Mark's advocate, and the discussion went around and around. But Paul was unswerving in his refusal.

As I envision the scene today, voices were raised. Paul and Barnabas, close friends and co-workers in faith, must have been bitterly disappointed with each other. Does such a rhubarb imply the absence of God? Is it proof that the Holy Spirit has left the building?

Believe it or not, we can disagree strongly and still be in God's will. Both men surely prayed about their stance. Who heard the wrong answer? Neither. Both stood firm, and eventually they went their separate ways—and that meant that God had *two* ways to bless instead of one. Barnabas and John Mark bore fruit in their direction, and Paul bore fruit in his own, with a new companion named Silas. Any planter will tell you that when it comes to planting fruit, you need more than one tree.

Therefore no one lost, everyone won. And years later, when Paul wrote his second latter to Timothy, he made a passing reference that put an exclamation point on the whole matter. Paul was near the end of his life this time. He was older and less robust. He asked Timothy to bring his special cloak to help keep out the cold. "Get Mark and bring him with you," he requested, "because he is helpful to me in my ministry" (2 Timothy 4:11). By this time, all three men were again partners in the gospel, and partakers of the wisdom that our Lord uses even our disagreements.

Do we serve a great God or what?

Most of the time we interpret any difference of opinion on any level as a sign that someone is out of God's will. Surely if every single one of us were completely committed to the Lord, we would all look, speak and act the same, right? Wouldn't we become carbon copies of one another—prefab followers?

I hope we can agree by now that the more we differ, the greater our potential for serving God together.

Friends of Distinction

These distinctions, of course, are all God's fault. He simply loves diversity and distinction. The Lord wants you to have fingerprints that aren't the same as anyone else's fingerprints. And that's more than simply his gift to law enforcement personnel. Something as tiny and temporary as a snowflake has its own absolutely unique identity. Billions of them fall quietly to earth, yet no two snowflakes are quite the same. Why? That's just how serious God is about the uniqueness of every single created thing.

Someone says, "They broke the mold when they made you." I have news: God doesn't use molds. He creates masterpieces, and every single one is precious and absolutely distinctive—living, thinking people far above and beyond the rest of his work.

There are some who try to bury the distinctives in order to simulate harmony. Perhaps you've heard someone say something like, "You know what? I don't even see color. I only see the body of Christ, where all the colors become one."

I say that fellow needs to get his eyes checked.

"When I look at you, Pastor Paul," someone says, "I don't see a black man."

"Why not?" I reply. "That's exactly what I am."

I know what he means; he doesn't see the *barrier* that all too often characterizes race relations in America. He doesn't see the kind of distinction that would get in the way of our fellowship. But breaking down the wall doesn't mean we're breaking down the distinctives, does it? It shouldn't. There are colors among us, and they are beautiful. They create a spectrum, as a rainbow does. They represent no mistake on the part of our Creator, but the mark of his artistry.

So when my friend says that he doesn't see my color, I reply, "I appreciate your heart. But don't blur the reality of who I am. We can be friends with our eyes open—differences and all."

One of my dear mentors, the late Bishop Benjamin Reid, told a story about this particular issue. Bishop Reid was a substantial man in many ways, including physically. When he boarded an airplane, he took a first-class seat because he needed the extra space. On one occasion, he was just getting comfortable in his seat when a tall, white gentleman in a cowboy hat slipped into the seat next to him.

The two men subtly sized each other up and began their flight without conversation.

As the plane took off, it was buffeted by heavy winds. There was a good bit of turbulence before the flight found its groove and settled into cruising altitude. The bishop sighed with relief and said, "Thank you, Jesus."

The cowboy turned sharply and blurted out, "*What* did you say?"

The bishop immediately thought, *How dare this man question my love for the Lord—my thanking God for smooth skies.* He went on thinking, *I bet he's wondering what a black man is doing in the first class section. Yes sir, I bet he's not only a bigot, but an atheistic bigot.*

The bishop had created a damning profile based on five minutes, four words, and a cowboy hat. Therefore he decided to answer the man's question defiantly. "I said thank you to Jesus," he said assertively.

"Well, hallelujah!" grinned the man in the cowboy hat, who immediately thrust out his right hand and identified himself as a pastor.

Bishop Reid, eyes wide, introduced himself as a fellow minister. And from that moment on, the flight passed very quickly as the two men chatted about the Lord and about their ministries, enjoying that amazing bond that can take hold so quickly between two people who serve the same Lord. The fellowship actually became so open and gratifying that both men began weeping—tears of joy over the goodness of God.

Flight attendants were nervous. After all, it's not every day that you see a huge black man and a white Texan crying together above the clouds! "Everything all right?" asked one.

The other man said, "Oh, yeah, everything's fine." With a big smile, he clapped the bishop on the shoulder and said, "This here is a long lost brother of mine."

The attendant cocked a dubious eyebrow. Seizing the moment, the man exclaimed: "Yep, we're brothers, and we have the same daddy!"

And of course, he spoke nothing but the truth. We have the same Daddy. We stand together at the foot of the cross, where we share one forgiveness, one hope, one limitless inheritance in Christ. When we let that fully sink in, we walk in joy. We walk in agreement.

2.

Acceptance: Walking in Equality

~~~~~~

The wonderful 1972 film *Sounder* tells the story of a poor family of sharecroppers. The family is black, the year is 1933, and the place is the Deep South.

In one scene, the mother and her son are walking along a country road, laughing at the jokes of their friend Ike, who has a witty line for every occasion. The three pedestrians pass a white church, just as the congregation is emerging from worship.

"What do they do in white churches, Mama?" asks Nathan Lee, the son.

His mother replies, "Same as we—they pray."

Ike adds, "You know, one time I walked into a white church down in Row County, just by mistake. To this day, I don't know how the devil I got out of there alive."

His two listeners want to hear what happened next. Ike continues, "I went home and did me some praying to the Lord. I said, 'Lord, I went into this white church down in Row and all I want you to tell me is how I ever got out of there in one piece.'"

Nathan Lee asks, "What did the Lord tell you, Ike?"

Ike replies that the Lord said, "I don't know, Ike—you're doing better than me. I've been tryin' to get in there for two hundred years, and I ain't made it yet."

Have you ever walked into a room and felt like a plump mouse at the National Cat Convention? Have you ever gone to a stadium and sat on the home side, dressed in the visiting team's colors?

I guess we've all been there at some point: a place where we don't feel accepted. The temperature of the room seems to drop about fifteen degrees as you walk in, and it seems as if every eye is fixed upon you. Few things in life are more uncomfortable. I've even preached in a setting or two like that.

On the other hand, think of a time when you knew you were among the "Best Folks in the World." I can't say exactly where that group is found; the answer is different for each of us. You might find it among your extended family, your grandparents, your aunts and uncles at Christmastime. It could be a club of some kind, a fraternity or sorority that is extremely close knit; *your* crowd, the people you'd rather hang with than any other group.

Maybe you've felt that wonderful spirit of togetherness with your old military unit at base camp, or simply in a Sunday school class that builds a family-like closeness over a number of years. The "Best Folks in the World" might turn up anywhere. The important thing is that feeling of being "where everybody knows your name," as the old television show put it.

There's a world of difference between those two extremes, isn't there? It's as wide as the difference between heaven and hell. Inside every one of us lies an intense yearning to feel acceptance, to feel the love. The extent to which we attain that acceptance goes a long way toward determining our happiness at any given time, in any given setting. Hard work under a hot sun can be something joyful when you're with the right people; the most comfortable mansion in the world can become a prison if it harbors an unhappy home.

We would really like our churches to be those oases of acceptance in this desert of a lonely world. If you read the second chapter of Acts, you get a picture of a fellowship that was just like that. The people were devoted to one another, they shared their lives and their earthly possessions, they enjoyed God, they prayed and preached, they cooked and dined, and subsequently their numbers were greater every day. People just kept wandering in to join the party and learn about the God who would sponsor such togetherness.

Yet you know it as well as I do: there's no room that can be colder than the sanctuary of a church. I'm not talking about temperature-cold. I'm talking about that invisible thermostat that measures the warmth of fellowship; the chill that is so apparent when someone drains the acceptance right out of the room.

All Things Being Equal

In the previous chapter we talked about walking together in agreement. We discussed the fact the difference between diversity and uniformity, or, in musical terms, between harmony and unison. It's a great day when we figure out that we can interlock comfortably in life despite our differences—in fact, that the differences are what a beautiful picture when the whole puzzle is assembled.

That's the first step: simply recognizing and affirming our differences. But we have to go the next miles, too. Someone is bound to say, "Okay, here's the deal with those other folks; you know the ones I mean. They are different, but that's okay. Let them have their own little room and their own little thing. Maybe they can even come to church at a whole different time, and we'll wave at each other as we pass by going and coming."

Walking in agreement doesn't mean walking in opposite directions, or toward different rooms in the building. It means walking *together* and sharing life *together*. So if the first step is to agree with one another, the second step is to accept one another as equals.

That can be a very difficult thing for some of us to do. For some reason, the human race loves look around and hash out the pecking order. When you're in high school, there are these little cliques or groups, and there are perceptions of social standings. Who is on the way up? Whose stock is sliding? That girl over there, she's a cheerleader and on the homecoming court: she's a ten. Bob over here, he's fairly popular, so we give him a seven. And Ahmad? He keeps to himself, and nobody likes him. He's with the "ones."

No one exactly publishes the standings, but we know what they are—and we spend a lot of time jockeying for a higher position by pushing someone else down.

You might remember the disciples getting caught up in their own pecking order. Jesus was leading them toward Jerusalem, warning them about the cross that lay ahead—but they were too busy arguing about who among them would sit at the right or left hand of Jesus when he came into his kingdom. Some of the mothers even got into the act. James and John, two brothers, brought Mama along, and she lobbied for her two boys to nail down the places of honor. Jesus understood that nails of a different kind were in store for him.

With all that Jesus had taught, all his words about the first being the last, the greatest becoming a servant—they had missed the message of treating everyone as an equal. The disciples had been just as amazed as the Pharisees by some of the company Jesus kept. He touched lepers. He frequented the homes of scandalous individuals, tax robbers, and outcasts. Jesus treated women as full fledged, God-blessed, human beings, though other men of the time treated women as property.

And children? The disciples thought they should be pushed aside when their important teacher was going to pass this way. But Jesus took their side; he came down to their level and listened. He accepted them.

With his dying breath, Jesus was all about acceptance, promising a thief a place beside him in paradise; asking God to forgive his murderers. Jesus didn't merely love, he loved to shocking lengths. He loved without restraint or restriction. You could do the very worst in the world to him, you could torture his body and curse his name, and he would love you all the same.

And he died to lay the ground for a place that kept that love and acceptance alive. He died so that you could enjoy total acceptance, and enjoy just as fully the total acceptance of others.

Chew on This

We've thought a little bit about how Jesus established incredible standards for loving acceptance. Think again about the circles in which we circulate, from home, to office, to school. What would those places be like if we learned to accept one another?

The Apostle Paul wanted the Roman church to consider that same possibility. Near the end of his letter to them, he wrote:

> *Accept him whose faith is weak, without passing judgment on disputable matters. One man's faith allows him to eat everything, but another man, whose faith is weak, eats only vegetables. The man who eats everything must not look down on him who does not, and the man who does not eat every-*

> *thing must not condemn the man who does, for God has accepted him. Who are you to judge someone else's servant? To his own master he stands or falls. And he will stand, for the Lord is able to make him stand. (Romans 14:1-4)*

The very first word in that passage is *accept*. In the original Greek language in which this letter was written, *accept* carries the meaning of *receive* or *take to oneself*. There is an implication of kindness and hospitality, such as when you speak about your best friend from childhood, and you say that his family "really took you in." You felt very comfortable and accepted in that home. Again in the Greek that Paul used, it was all about someone going out of his way to make someone feel welcome.

There are people in this world who are specially gifted in that area. Twenty different people might believe themselves to be that person's best friend. It's not difficult at all to be friendly and welcoming when we have something to gain from it. If your boss from work, who decides your salary, is coming to dinner, it's amazing what a delightful host you can be.

What Paul is talking about is treating everyone else the same way—including people you don't even like.

Let's take a closer look at the specific situation behind his words. The church in Rome, like most of the new congregations across the Mediterranean world, had an uneasy mix of people who were bonded only by their attraction to Jesus. Jews, of course, were present, because when Paul came to town to preach the gospel, he started in the synagogue. The Jews continued all their traditional practices even after they became Christians. It was just ingrained in them to eat certain foods, to honor certain holidays, and to uphold certain practices.

Gentile Christians, of course, didn't share that tradition. As Paul explained it to them, they didn't need to be Jewish to follow Jesus, even though Jesus had been Jewish. They simply needed to accept his teachings and his gift of salvation. This became quite a controversy even among the disciples back in Jerusalem: Christianity emerged from Judaism, but where was the line of separation between them?

So now you can imagine two believers from Rome, sharing their midday meal. One opens his lunch box and pulls out a piece of meat that has been prepared in a certain way. His friend's eyes grow wide as he says, "You going to eat that?"

"Why?" asks the first man, taking a big bite. "You want some?"

"Most certainly *not!*" replies the horrified friend. "Can't you see that it's a scrap from idol worship?"

"Sure," he replies, wiping his chin with a napkin.

"Well, it's . . . it's unholy. *Ungodly.*"

"To you, maybe," says the first man. "To me, it's a fine piece of veal. Jesus saves me because of his grace, not my diet."

The second man pushes his chair violently from the table and leaves the room.

Becoming a Grindstone

How would you resolve such a dispute? These were common in the early church. Paul's point is that it's more a matter of the heart than the stomach. He would now enter the room, sit down with that first man, and say, "Just for the record, you were right . . . and wrong. Yes, you are truly free in Christ to eat any healthy food you desire. You're no longer bound by law and ceremony."

"I knew it!" The first man attempts a high five, but Paul leaves him hanging.

"On the other hand, you were wrong in that you offended your brother."

"I don't get it." If I wasn't doing anything wrong, why is my lunch any of his business?"

You know where this is going. We *are* each other's business. Our goal is to sharpen one another, as we read in Proverbs 27:17: "As iron sharpens iron, so one man sharpens another." In other words, just as a grindstone would sharpen a good steak knife, we would make each other wiser and better people simply from our fellowship. Sometimes, however, we focus on ourselves instead of our brother or sister. We don't sharpen one another as much as wear each other down.

Paul's advice in Romans 14 is that neither the ceremonially oriented believer nor the "liberated" one has any cause to look down on the other. Those are passing things, temporary issues, but our friends are *eternal souls* like us. We are to treat one another as an eternal soul, a child of God, an heir of his kingdom. And when your path crosses an heir to a great fortune, do you point out all your disagreements with that person? It's more likely that you'd be on your best behavior, ready to please.

That's exactly how you should treat your fellow believer, Paul tells us, because he or she is an heir to the most awesome fortune imaginable—the kingdom and power of God.

The problem is that we simply refuse to see each other through that lens. We look at people and see the flaws—or what seem like flaws from our perspective. (Remember what Jesus said about that? Better check your eyes, because there may be some object blocking your own vision that is larger than the speck you're pointing out in your brother or sister.)

We do these things in our mind: We decide on the pecking order, then we begin rooting out those we feel don't belong. That fellow over in the next pew, for instance—he pulled in front of me in the church parking lot last Sunday, when I was trying to hurry to the cafeteria. That woman in front of me—

I just know she isn't hearing a word of the sermon; I know because I've been watching her closely the entire time!

My friend, the composition of the church is a no-voting proposition. I know what that means because my parents held a few non-voting meetings in our household when I was growing up. There were certain things that were non-negotiable. Think back to that fledgling church in Rome. It lived each day of its life a centurion or two away from extinction. Its mission was a perilous one. Yet here was controversy over what kinds of meat could be put on the lunchroom menu. If the church began dividing on such lines, and sending one party or the other away, then Christianity would not survive in that city.

Look around at your own church. Has the way its members practice love and acceptance resulted in a powerful move of God that is transforming the community around it? Are people seeing an incredible harmony that's so attractive and God-inspired they're beating down your door to let them in? In most of our churches, that's not the case. In fact, some churches are so preoccupied with their fights, factions, and fault-finding that they haven't noticed the stark contrast between what they proclaim and what they practice. And what's worse, some probably wouldn't care if they did. But if our witness is going to impact our 21st century world, we must take heed to the exhortation of a 1st century apostle and build bridges where walls currently stand.

Not in My Kingdom

In 1984, When a dazzling group of musical celebrities gathered in one studio to record a benefit song, "We Are the World," the producer, Quincy Jones, put out a sign that said, "Check your ego at the door." He knew that any time you assemble world class performers, you're bound to have world class pride and world class stubbornness. If Bruce

Springsteen gets into an argument with Lionel Richie, and Elton John clashes with Diana Ross, you'll probably never get to the recording process. The sign was Quincy's way of saying, "Not in my studio."

That's what God says when he assembles all the princes and princesses who are the heirs to his kingdom. We want to be treated like royalty, but we don't want to extend the same privileges. Therefore we begin attacking one another. God says, "Not in my kingdom!"

In his kingdom, it doesn't matter what background anyone comes from. It's a party where everyone is invited.

In his kingdom, no one is more special than anyone else. We all stand at the foot of the cross, where the ground is level.

In his kingdom, you are loved spectacularly, infinitely, unconditionally—but so is everyone else. Can you live with that?

In his kingdom, there are children and old-timers; hymn-lovers and hip-hoppers; people of every complexion, every economic class, every temperament. Yes, it can get messy at times, but so does making coal into diamonds—which is exactly what the Spirit of God is doing when he brings us all together. We think we know the best way to clean up the "mess," but God says, "Not in my kingdom."

God says it of his kingdom because it works in *any* kingdom. Acceptance improves any place where people come together. The business office where you work is a much more pleasant place when co-workers accept one another, forgive one another, drop their demands upon one another, and simply resolve to live with the grace by which Christ has already accepted us. The neighborhood where you live is a much more relaxing place to return at the end of the day when you treat everyone on your street exactly as you want to be treated. And what about your family? You love your family—how could acceptance be an issue there?

The truth is that many children don't feel accepted, and many parents could afford to learn how to express their love to their children. The love is there; it simply needs to be felt. A son may feel unaccepted by his father if he doesn't make the football or baseball team. A daughter may feel unaccepted if she doesn't grow into her mother's idea of what she is supposed to be. Loving our children means loving them unconditionally—a word that simply means "no matter what."

Our children must understand that no matter what happens, no matter what mistakes they can make, they will never be unworthy of our love. This is the pattern God has set for us, and he wants us to model it in our own relationships. If your child comes home with an F in mathematics, the grade is unacceptable—but the child is not. It seems simple to us, but we must make sure our children see the difference, too.

Earning the Right to Be Heard

While we're thinking about parenting, let's take a look at another reason that acceptance is essential. Without it, who will listen to us?

As a parent, your job is to speak truth into the life of your child. All the time your child is growing from infancy to the threshold of adulthood, you are teaching, training, transferring the treasures of your life's education. This includes your values, your judgments, your spiritual beliefs, and everything you want to pour into the ears and the minds of your children. There is a saying that is a cliché, but it's a cliché because it is true: No one cares about how much we know until they know how much we care.

All of the significant individuals who have molded you, from your parents and your teachers on down the line, have been people who accepted you and loved you. They transformed your life with your permission, because you knew how they felt about you. It's true in professional life, too; many of us can point to a mentor or difference-maker early in our career. This person cared; he or she reached outside the limitations of duty and assignment to help us on their own time, and with their own spirit and love. We never forget such people. We heard them because they earned the right to be heard.

If you want your children to hear and apply your teaching, they must feel total acceptance, unconditional love. Sometimes we sit down with them and really unload a lot of negative feelings about their life and lifestyle, their friends, their culture, and whatever else boils up through our frustration. What our children hear is a lack of acceptance of who they are. We have to learn to guide them from a foundation of caring and acceptance that they can always feel securely. When we force them to sit down, barking, "You're going to listen and listen now, because I said so," you're not going to accomplish much other than increase anger.

The connection is all-important. Imagine asking your daughter to bring her best friend to meet you for the first time. The friend sits down, you smile, and you say, "I want to teach you all about life, just as I've taught my daughter. What I'm about to tell you is time-tested—my parents taught me, and their parents before them. It's biblically sound and approved by nine out of ten parenting experts. Just stop me if you have any questions." Then you begin expounding all your principles and values.

Why would you fail so miserably? Your daughter's friend is likely to wonder, "Who does this fellow think he is?" You aren't connected. You haven't earned the right to be heard, so you cannot speak truth into that particular life, no matter *how* true the truth is.

And think about this: Why is it that your best, most logically air-tight arguments often fail to win people over? Sure, you have all the points neatly outlined, a-b-c, 1-2-3. It could be a political argument, an argument about faith, or a dispute about who is really the best running back in the National Football League. It doesn't matter what the subject is, nor your personal credentials for arguing the matter. Sometimes it's just a case of someone's stubbornness; but more often that we'd like to realize, the obstacle is relational rather than rational.

As we all know, arguments lead us to speak more rapidly and listen less attentively every moment. That's why James advises, "Everyone should be quick to listen, slow to speak and slow to become angry" (James 1:19). Nothing is accomplished but the heightening of anger and frustration between two people. What happens, however, when you show the body language of caring—listening, eye contact, gentle voice—it's amazing how much better your points will be taken. People accept your wisdom when you accept them.

Condone or Condemn?

Let's stop and make an important distinction. Lest you think I'm espousing permissiveness in parenting, hear this clearly: To accept does not mean to condone.

If a hurting person comes to your church, it's always right to accept the individual; it's not always right to accept that individual's actions. If you provided comfort and assistance to a drug addict, you would not be endorsing the drug use—only God's love for the user.

Was Jesus endorsing the dishonesty of Zacchaeus, who cheated people out of extra tax money? Was he endorsing the lifestyles of the "sinners" whose homes he was accused of frequenting? He didn't condone, but he loved people and called them to lives that were better. He does the same for you and for me.

You might remember the story from John 8, when the Pharisees stepped forward with a woman caught in adultery, and dumped her at the feet of Jesus. They were using her as a case study, hopefully a trap to make Jesus look either as judgmental as them, or as licentious as the Romans, who forbade such an execution. The Pharisees frankly hoped it was a no-win situation for Jesus, because he was annoying them more each day. They wanted him to choose between legalism and liberalism, missing the fact that God is neither.

Of course, if these Pharisees were so consumed by the mission of hunting down every sin, we must ask about the man in the adultery scenario. Where was he? This woman was "caught in the act," we're told, so presumably the man was right there, too. Obviously they set him free, while they carried the woman into the public square for public humiliation. He may even have been among the rubber-neckers in this scene.

Jesus didn't need a review of the laws of Moses—he knew every word—but the Pharisees reminded him anyway: it was on the books that this woman should be stoned. So what was he going to do?

What he did was to stoop down and write in the sand, increasing the suspense of the scene. The Bible doesn't tell us what he wrote, it makes a careful point of telling us that he did. Perhaps he was writing the names of onlookers and their respective sins; perhaps he wrote his own accusation, leveled at the accusers.

We don't know. But as the mob continued to press him for an answer, Jesus invited them to apply the punishment on this basis: Let the sinless one throw the first stone. Then he continued what he was writing in the dirt. Finally, when the crowd had drifted away without casting a pebble, Jesus told the woman that if no one else condemned her, neither did he. But hear his final words: "Go now and leave your life of sin" (John 8:11).

He did not condone, neither did he condemn. He accepted the child of God and rejected the ungodly behavior.

The important point is that the first is the seed, the second is the bloom. Real change grows from an atmosphere of acceptance. Do you think the woman was more likely to listen to the advice of the Pharisees or Jesus? The first earned her fear, while the second earned her love and gratitude. We don't condemn, we don't condone, but we offer compassion. Then we have the opportunity to make something good happen in someone's life.

Hardcore Acceptance

Someone says, "But I must serve God and take my stand against sin! He is a holy God, and I must hate sin as he does!"

Yes, but part of the holiness of God is holy love. His hatred of sin is absolute, but so is his love of every child he created on this earth. If you want to take a stand for God, take a stand by showing his love. We have more than enough judgment and self-righteousness already. Wrath and judgment we can comprehend, but perfect love is a difficult concept. Here's a way to think about it.

God's acceptance is like this: He refused to watch our sin from the distance of heaven, because we were destroying ourselves and each other with it. So he clothed himself in flesh and became one of us. He came into the world and lived just as you would expect God to live on this earth. He taught people the truth, he helped and healed, he showed the best way to live at every moment. And never once did he commit a sin himself.

Then he offered himself up to receive the worst treatment we can imagine. Not only did he not deserve it, but nobody does. Having given the world nothing but goodness and light, he was beaten and tortured for hours, stripped and humiliated before jeering crowds, nailed by the hands and feet to crude crossbeams, and left there to die a slow, horrible death of asphyxiation.

As he was dying that death, feeling that pain, and fighting for his last puffs of air, he then forgave the men who did it to him. He looked out upon the guards and the thugs who laughed at his agony and said, "Forgive them, for they don't realize what they're doing."

Now I ask you: Is that the attitude, and are those the words, of a liberal, permissive parent who is soft on sin? Or has he earned the right to accept sinners, and to ask that we do the same?

That's hardcore love and forgiveness, my friend. There is nothing cheap about it. When we realize the height and depth of his love for us, we are stopped short. Then comes the really hard part—we come to the realization that we are called to live out that love ourselves. Paul puts it into words:

Your attitude should be the same as that of Christ Jesus:

Who, being in very nature God,
did not consider equality with God something to
be grasped,
but made himself nothing,
taking the very nature of a servant,
being made in human likeness.
And being found in appearance as a man,
he humbled himself
and became obedient to death—
even death on a cross!
Therefore God exalted him to the highest place
and gave him the name that is above every name,
that at the name of Jesus every knee should bow,
in heaven and on earth and under the earth,

and every tongue confess that Jesus Christ is Lord,
to the glory of God the Father.
—Philippians 2:5-11

"Your attitude should be the same." Those are frightening words, aren't they? Jesus paid the highest imaginable price, and now receives the highest possible glory. You and I can never love with the perfection that he loved—but we can do our best, can't we?

Sometimes we're going to have our bad days. We're not going to love with our full potential through the enabling power of the Holy Spirit. But that's the great thing about this principle. We, too, are accepted. We fall under that forgiveness that Jesus offered from the cross.

We are still under construction, you and me. He hasn't gotten us quite to the place where he wants us to be, but he's getting us there one step at a time.

A Soft Place to Fall

I believe the Lord wants us to become people who are good at building bridges rather than reinforcing walls. He wants his church to become a place where people can go when there is nowhere else to go; a place where people can say, "Here I am, with all my problems. I want to hear what God's will is for my life. I need his grace, and I need to walk with people who are also experiencing it."

Several years ago, after an exploring membership orientation, a young man pulled me aside and asked if he could have a word with me.

We sat down to talk. The young man looked very nervous as he said, "Pastor, I want to join the church . . ."

I said, "Well that's great! We're blessed to have you."

"But I struggle with being sexually attracted to men" he continued, watching my eyes.

I nodded for him to continue.

"A tendency, you know what I mean," he said. "I've fought this battle for awhile. I love being here, but I don't want to mess up your church. Do you know what I mean?"

I smiled. "I think I do."

The young man said, "I want to serve God, and I want to live a life pleasing to him. But I don't want to mess up your church."

I said, "Brother, it's already messed up."

Those weren't the words he expected to hear. His eyes were wide.

"You're too late," I said, "if you think you'll be the one to come here and mess up our church. I've got news for you. You're hundreds of members too late, as a matter of fact!"

He smiled at that thought.

I continued, "My friend, you'll discover quickly that this place isn't a country club that exists for the spiritually well-to-do; it's a hospital. It's not for those who want to believe that they've already attained perfection, but for people sick with sin and who really want to get well and experience the transforming power of God."

I had the happy task of explaining to that young man that in God's eyes, he was totally forgiven in Christ, in whom there is no condemnation. There was going to be a lot of work, of course, because the Holy Spirit is always working in every single one of us, to conform us to the image of Christ. His challenge would probably not disappear as if by magic. But he was among friends who would walk with him as he walked with Christ.

I reached for a membership profile and handed it to my friend to fill out. I said, "You're welcome here, brother. Commit yourself to building godly relationships with fellow believers and growing in grace, and you'll be amazed at how Christ, through the power of the Holy Spirit, will give you a shining testimony."

I have heard it said that the church should be "a soft place to fall," and that sounds just about right to me. The church should be a place where people can come when they are weary, when they are wounded, when they can barely walk. The world is filled to capacity with hurting souls who are looking for a soft place to fall, a friendly place to heal, and a hopeful place to start again.

Can we build such a place, or is it only a pipe dream? Can we create doors so wide that any hungry soul can walk through them, walls as sturdy as our love for those people, and a foundation that is unshakably built on the uncompromised truth of God's Word? Can we raise an army of saints armed with love rather than legalism? Can we stand for both grace and truth simultaneously?

Call me an idealist, because I believe we can. We can love people like Christ did—neither condemning the sinner nor condoning the sin, but rather pointing them to the Savior who has the power to forgive our sins and cleanse us from all unrighteousness.

And I'm convinced that as churches will commit to love people in a Christ-like way, we will be entrusted with an incredible harvest of souls in these critical days before our Lord returns.

3.

Allowance: Leaving Room for Honest Differences

There is a rather odd comedian named Emo Philips who has one particularly good story. He tells about an occasion when he was getting to know a new acquaintance. Somehow the subject of church came up, and he asked, "Are you Protestant or Catholic?"

His new friend replied, "Protestant."

"Me too!" smiled Emo. "What franchise?"

The man answered, "Baptist."

"Me too!" said Emo, clapping him on the shoulder. "Northern Baptist or Southern Baptist?"

"Northern Baptist," qualified his friend.

"Me too!" Emo laughed. Small world!

It continued along these lines until the comedian got it narrowed down this far: "Northern Conservative Fundamentalist Baptist, Great Lakes Region, Council of 1879—or Northern Conservative Fundamentalist Baptist, Great Lakes Region, Council of 1912?"

The friend quickly replied, "The second one."

Emo Philips snapped, "Die, heretic!"

Anybody who knows a little bit about the history of our faith—or has even kept an eye on church behavior—has to smile a bit sadly when he hears that story. We seem to be very good at drawing lines in the sand. Sometimes it's over the question of who Jesus is. That's a big one, and worth some accurate line drawing. Other times it's over the color of the sanctuary carpet, or whether or not the choir should wear robes. Those cases are not worth an ounce of worry.

In the last couple of chapters we have talked about accepting one another, walking in unity and equality. Now it gets a little interesting, doesn't it? Once we've begun to walk together, we might begin to talk together. We're going to learn that we're not carbon copies of one another, and we will have to decide how much slack to cut each other.

You and I are seeing this issue come up more often, and in a way it's because the church is doing its job. We are opening our doors to people who know very little about our faith and traditions. Now I'm certain it was very comfortable back in the heyday of our parents or grandparents, in, say, the 1950s, when so much of our country not only went to church but agreed on how to do things. The music sounded just as it had for many years, and everyone knew the rules. There's something to be said for that level of unity, but at some point, many of our churches stopped reaching out and fulfilling our most essential task: winning new people for Christ.

Now it's a new day. With all our little problems, at least we're starting to be conscious of people who didn't get the memo on what to believe about the Second Coming, or whether you can bring a cup of coffee into the sanctuary. (What would Mom and Dad have thought about that one?) In our church there are people who love the music, who listen intently to the preaching, but bless their hearts, they haven't gotten squeezed into our cookie cutters yet! Sometimes they do things and believe things that make us a little tense, don't they?

I say this is a part of the church doing its job because I find the very same situation in the New Testament. The very first Christians, the ones who were either disciples or taught by them, were all Jewish. Jewish laws and regulations were part of their tradition, so it was natural for them to carry that over to their new faith in Christ. Then here came Paul, who had a new vision for the boundaries of this faith. He believed that non-Jewish people would want to know Jesus, too. And those non-Jewish people didn't know the finer points of kosher diet or Sabbath law. You couldn't blame them for asking, "Circumcision—mind telling me what that has to do with inviting Jesus into my heart?"

Yet Paul had friends who insisted that these gentiles (as the non-Jews were called) must be circumcised; that they must eat exactly what God's chosen people had eaten since the days of Moses, and that they must honor every Hebrew ceremonial tradition.

Do you see the connection? The new fellow in the back pew says, "I don't even own a tie! And you're telling me I have to wear one every Sunday? Can I find this in the Bible somewhere?"

His wife says, "I visited the Bible study class, and people started to talk about politics. Everyone was for the same candidate, and it seemed as if they believed that everyone who is a Christian would be for their candidate and their political party. Did Jesus have position papers on all these issues?"

At this point we begin to stammer, "Well, that's just kind of how we do things, that's all." And somewhere, there may even be a spoken or unspoken message: "If you can't handle the way we do things, my friend, there are other churches in town."

Yet I think our churches are beginning to look a little bit like the ones in the first century. I think that's a very good thing; notice I didn't say it was a very *easy* thing. The point is that, as we've already seen, God isn't looking for uniformity but unison. He just loves to look upon our gatherings and see men and women; the young and the aged; the rich and the poor; and every skin color he has created. He loves it because he knows that only love, only *his* fabulous love, can join and sustain the harmony of lovely diversity.

Hung Up for Hang-ups

We all have our different hang-ups. For me it may be some doctrinal issue. For you it might be appearances or politics or practices. C. S. Lewis once pointed out that it's interesting how we choose to evaluate other people's flaws. He said that it was easy to criticize that acquaintance who drinks a little too much, as long as you yourself aren't particularly drawn to that temptation. But it could be that you're the one who can't quite push away from the dinner table. If so, you're probably not too critical of the sin of gluttony. As a matter of fact, while you're whispering about the brother who needs help with his drinking, have you given any thought to the sin of gossiping?

That's why Jesus warned us not to get hung up on the speck in someone else's eye when there's a chunk of wood in our own. We all have our hang-ups, but the fact is that Jesus was hung up for every hang-up we could possibly imagine, and some we couldn't. For some reason, we're on the lookout for perfect people to be our friends, our spouses, our pastors, our employees. We want to sand away their rough edges, or what we think are rough edges, until we get them to our liking. But who will sand away our own rough edges?

Jesus has it a little differently. He isn't looking for perfect people. He is looking for people to give perfect love. No edge is too rough. No flaw renders any of us unacceptable. He wants us just the way we are, and he wants us to look upon each other the same way. His death, burial, and resurrection are enough to save every one of us, and yet not a one of us deserves it. Can we walk away from such a gift without loving each other in a new and more accepting way? Must we hang on to our hang-ups?

Jesus told another story about a man who owed the debt of a lifetime to a wealthy official. It was like owing a lottery award that he'd never won—millions of dollars. We're not told how he ever got into that kind of debt, and this was a long time before Las Vegas. At any rate, the official had the debtor brought forward. Instead of throwing him into prison for the rest of the poor man's natural life, he wrote off the debt entirely. "Go on," he said. "You're free."

It was a shocking display of grace and forgiveness. The man couldn't believe his good fortune. He ran through the streets rejoicing—until he met a man who owed him a couple of bucks. This was no massive debut, but only a matter of "chump change." Yet the newly liberated debtor became red in the face, grabbed this other man by the scruff of the neck, and demanded that the poor fellow *pay up!*

You know where this is leading. The high and mighty official got wind of this episode, and he couldn't believe his ears. He immediately reinstituted the lottery-sized debt and had the unappreciative debtor thrown in prison after all.

Now here's the question. Why do you think Jesus would talk about a debt so large, so impossible to build up? He did it because he was talking about something other than money: our inner debt before God. In soul dollars, we're way, way below break-even. We all know this. We are so flawed, so imperfect, so filled with unfitting thoughts and disappointing deeds that we could never truly earn a second of this wonderful life he grants us each day on this beautiful planet. We owe him everything and can pay nothing. Yet he says to us, "Go on. You're free." And whenever we go on about our merry way only to make silly demands of other people, only to revert to our hang-ups for which he was hung up, instead of passing on the grace we've been handed—we are insulting the goodness of God we never deserved in the first place.

I want you to think right now about someone you just cannot love. Don't worry, you won't have to think long; God will put the name right into your mind.

See what I mean? Hold onto that name and the picture of that person in your mind. That's someone Jesus gave his precious, perfect life to save. In soul dollars, Jesus was way above the break-even point—the only human being who ever was—and he didn't decide he could not love that person. He said that person was accepted; could come into the family. And the way I see it, if Jesus says that person can come into the family, than I don't get a say in it.

Go Forth and Change That Diaper

I've heard it said that you pick your friends, but you're stuck with your relatives. On one occasion when Jesus identified the second greatest commandment—to love our neighbor—someone threw out this question: "Sure, but who is our neighbor?"

The man thought he had Jesus right there; busted him on a question that had no answer, right? Nobody has ever invented an official neighbor detector, something you can pull out of the glove compartment and check when you see someone hurt by the side of the road. So Jesus talked about that injured fellow at the roadside. He basically said, in so many words, that we don't get to choose our neighbor either. We never even ask that man's question. God has already filled out the neighbor slate. You're looking at it whenever you meet someone; it's a divine appointment. God brought you someone to love and to accept, and hopefully someone to love and accept you. It's in your job description, and you can't cross it out. Why would anyone even want to?

Those familiar with my family know that my parents had four children in reasonably rapid succession, one after the other: four stair steps, a nice, even number. Ten years passed, and the oldest of us were teenagers; I was 14 years old. We were past the kid stuff in our family. Highchairs and cribs were packed away.

Or so we thought. About that time, my parents went on a vacation cruise and got frisky. Nature took its course, and a few months later, they gathered us for an emergency family meeting at the dining room table.

We didn't see this one coming at all, and had no idea what the meeting was all about. Why did Mom have that look of discomfort on her face? Finally she simply said, "I'm going to have another child."

We just stared at her, jaws clattering on the floor. No way. These old people had up and made another baby? We figured Jonah and the whale was an easier story to believe. We looked from the face of our mother, who seemed perplexed, to the face of our father, whose face was proud, beaming. The look in his eyes said, "Yep, yep. I still got it."

We often had voting meetings at that dining room table, very democratic. This session was not one of those. We had no say in whether there was going to be a new family member; Mom and Dad cast the only ballots on that one. They had voted back on the cruise ship.

Months later, my mother arrived home from the hospital and put a little bundle into my arms. "This is your little brother Kenny," she said. "Go and change his diaper."

That's the story of God's kingdom, my friend. *Here's your brother; go change his diaper.* When my mother handed that tiny little guy to me, I wasn't about to say, "Don't look at me; I didn't vote for him."

And when God brings you to me, I'm not going to say it to him, either—no matter how much of a mess you've made!

And here's something to think about. Sometimes you, too, need someone to help clean up your own mess.

"Disputable Matters"

Let's take another look at the words of Paul in Romans 14:

Accept him whose faith is weak, without passing judgment on disputable matters. One man's faith allows him to eat everything, but another man, whose faith is weak, eats only vegetables. The man who eats everything must not look down on him who does not, and the man who does not eat everything must not condemn the man who does, for God has accepted him. Who are you to judge someone else's servant? To his own master he stands or falls. And he will stand, for the Lord is able to make him stand.

(Romans 14:1-4)

Paul coins an interesting phrase here: "disputable matters," those little gray areas of life that are up for interpretation. You make the call. Now the question is, what is a disputable matter? The answer itself, of course, is a disputable matter. Everybody draws their boundaries just a little differently.

Therefore Paul goes on to give us a couple of examples. In the second verse, he offers the example of one's chosen diet. For us, this is seldom a matter for the church today. We do know those who eat fish on Fridays, but many of us would be more likely to classify food choice as an issue of health and fitness. Yet in the first century, and particularly wherever Hebrew tradition came into play, the daily menu was a matter of serious theology. The rules had been set forth long ago.

In verse five, Paul adds another hot button topic: the issue of religious holidays.

One man considers one day more sacred than another; another man considers every day alike. Each one should be fully convinced in his own mind. He who regards one day as special, does so to the Lord. He who eats meat, eats to the Lord, for he gives thanks to God; and he who abstains, does so to the Lord and gives thanks to God. For none of us lives to himself alone and none of us dies to himself alone. If we live, we live to the Lord; and if we die, we die to the Lord. So, whether we live or die, we belong to the Lord.

(Romans 14:5-8)

We see this one a little more often today, with our culture of diversity in the workplace. Every spiritual tradition has its own special days, and even within one faith there are specific holidays set forth—one group observes Ash Wednesday at Easter time, for example, while another isn't sure what that's all about. What we call liturgical calendars are very important for some churches; for others, not so much. The first American settlers in Plymouth, Massachusetts, those people known as the Pilgrims, didn't even celebrate Christmas or Easter. They associated holy days with worldliness. That was their stance on a "disputable matter."

What Paul says here is crucial. All disagreements are not created equal. Some are worth pursuing with love and respect, and on others we agree to disagree. Whatever your take is, Paul tells us, be fully convinced; don't sit on any fences. But be sure to allow for honest disagreement. That means that if you come to me and tell me that Jesus is not the Son of God, I'm going to want to change your mind about that. Hopefully I will not grab you, get you into a painful wrestling hold, and intimidate you into a confession of faith; friendly persuasion is more what I have in mind. But for me, and I would hope for all Christians, the divinity of Christ is not a disputable matter.

But what day do you set aside for public worship? Not everybody reserves Sunday for that distinction. Do you believe that our election in Christ is conditional or unconditional? Christians have disputed that one for hundreds of years, and not always peacefully—but there's room for loving disagreement. Can a Christian smoke a cigarette? Go to an R-rated movie? Which should receive more of the church budget, local missions or international ones? Can a Christian get a tattoo? To what extent should a pastor get involved in political issues?

We could have some lively discussions on any of these questions, and I hope we could do so with open minds, humor, and mutual respect. But not a single one of them is a test of fellowship. Paul says that food and holidays fall under that same category. Find your stance and take your position, but hold your fire. Coexist in love and acceptance with those who differ.

In other words, I'm not going to worry over whether or not you make the final cut for heaven based on your answer to any question in the paragraph above. Every one of them is a disputable matter, and we need to make room for honest disagreements. You see, if anything was ever certain, this is: People will be arguing about those things long after you and I are gone, and in most cases, minds will not be changed. Friendships will be disrupted, churches will be distracted, and the world will be severely unimpressed—but minds will not be changed. That's why we need to pick our battles with incredible discernment and wisdom.

Just Grow Up

It's just possible that there are times when we make the idea of spiritual growth more complicated than it really is. For example: If we want to become the people God intends us to be, we simply need to grow up emotionally.

Read your New Testament and you'll see what I mean. Jesus, Paul, John, Peter and the other writers are always laying out standards for living, often with "one another" attached, and they always seem to make the connection to emotional maturity. Have you ever studied the list of "one anothers" in the New Testament? *Accept* one another. *Encourage* one another. *Love* one another. *Forgive* one another. *Bear with* one another. These are all things that true grownups do—people who have grown to their full height in spirit as well as in body. Wherever Jesus went, he was surrounded by religious experts who knew all the answers, had memorized every footnote in thousands of pages of ancient, sacred dogma. Yet those experts could be unbelievably petty. They could see a blind man receive his sight, a leper fully cured, and then feel no joy because it happened on the wrong day of the week. What kind of person could not be moved by a miracle of Jesus? Someone who hasn't grown up emotionally, that's who.

The Pharisees were a case study of what happens to people who cannot allow for honest differences. Such people are always drawing a line in the sand and retreating behind it. Finally they have drawn the lines so sharply that they've painted themselves into a corner—created a personal prison that lets no one inside. It must be lonely to live that way. "My way or the highway" is their creed, but it seems like a *low* way to me. The King's Highway is the way of acceptance and love, and it's a way that distinguishes between what is truly important and what is ultimately inconsequential. It draws a few essential lines, but it builds many bridges.

I'll admit that this takes some careful thinking sometimes. Life is filled with judgment calls, and they're not always cut and dried. You may have to tell your friend, "Let me think on that one, and I'll get back to you." That's another gadget we need, much like the neighbor detector: a dispute-ometer, we could call it. It could give us a reading on just how important we should consider a question.

For example, I've heard people say that the virgin birth of Christ is a disputable matter. I would beg to differ there, because that's one that deeply touches the divine nature of Jesus Christ. If he was born to a normal set of parents like you and me, then we have no Savior, just another human leader, and one born in sin. My sins and yours could only be taken care of by someone qualified to do so. He would have to be from heaven and be without sin. We believe that our Lord and Savior was fully human but also fully divine, and every major Christian creed from the beginning has included his birth from a virgin. So that's a question upon which I'll have to be insistent, with all love and respect. If you have a question about it, I would love to spend time with you and explain in greater detail. But you're not going to change my mind on that one.

I believe we serve the one true God, that His son was crucified to death, then rose bodily from the grave, and that he will one day return. I believe that the Bible is God's inspired Word, and that heaven and hell are on the other side of this life. Those are theological essentials; non-negotiable items to be embraced by me and everyone who would follow Jesus Christ and be counted among his faithful. It needs to be said that, just as there are some who would fight over every trivial issue, but there are others who count no issue as particularly worth defending. This is ultimately just as dangerous, because if we stand for nothing, we might fall for anything.

The fact is that Jesus never said, "I'm just another in a series of options for your lifestyle, so place me alongside Buddha, Vishnu, and Muhammad." Jesus was not politically correct but amazingly bold: He claimed to be the one and only Son of God, and he said that nobody could come to the Father but by him. If he was wrong about that, then he's not the "wise teacher" that people want to label him. He drew a line right there, and that's not a line you or I could afford to wipe away or redraw or redirect. People have died for that line that he drew, and rightfully so, because Jesus himself was the first to die for it.

If you are a church member, you can probably find a doctrinal statement that lays out the essentials of its beliefs. If it's a mainstream Christian church, you'll notice some of the issues I've just mentioned: God's triune (three-person) nature, Christ's death, resurrection, and eventual return, his full humanity and full divinity, our Bible as God's revelation, the place of the church, and a few others. It concerns me that many people would be at a loss to tell you the specifics of what they believe. Do you study the label before you take a pill from the medicine cabinet? Do you read the ingredients of your groceries, or do you just say, "This looks like food"? Details, man! We need to be informed, to know what we put inside us whether it's drug, dinner, or devotion. Then we know exactly where those boundaries lie, and we don't need to be so uptight when we encounter differences among ourselves.

Lines Within Lines

But it gets even more interesting. Let's take one of those essentials. We believe that Christ will return to this earth again, and "he will come to judge the living and the dead," as one creed phrases it. We call that, of course, the Second Coming.

77

So that one's taken care of, nice and neat. Every Christian now knows exactly what to believe and where to draw the line on the Second Coming, right? Wrong, of course. If you've been around Christians for more than just a few minutes, you know how much room is left for interpretation even when we agree that there is indeed a Second Coming. When will Jesus come back? And will there be a secret rapture of the church or not? Will there be a literal battle of Armageddon or should certain apocalyptic passages be taken figuratively? My friends, even if I took the rest of this book and added five sequels and an interactive DVD, I couldn't provide neat answers that every Bible teacher would agree with. But I could start plenty of arguments!

You see, even within the essentials there is room for honest disagreement. On any item of discourse, you can believe that Jesus gave us just as much information as he wanted us to have. It's important that we know and affirm he is coming again. The details are to be announced. You'll be the first to know, and until then you can choose your own interpretation. Just don't hit your friend over the head with your King James Bible if he doesn't agree. There is a wonderful cartoon that appeared in *Leadership Journal* a few years ago. It was drawn by the cartoonist Rob Portlock and it shows a group of ministers entering the gates of heaven. They are surprised to see several doors. One is marked "Premillennial." Another is marked "Postmillennial." Still another is "Amillennial." These are three common interpretations of the End Times. The ministers are selecting the doors that match their beliefs. But we, the readers, can see the other side of the doors. Once you walk through one of them, your path merges with the other two, and everyone walks together to go see Jesus.

I like that, because it says there is room for honest disagreement, we may take slightly different paths, but at the end of the day we can all walk together to see our Lord. Now if you changed that cartoon and had the doors saying

Christianity, Islam, Buddhism, and Hinduism, but the paths still converged, I would no longer like that cartoon. People are often trying to do that with faith these days, saying that (as Linus put it in the *Peanuts* comic strip), "it doesn't matter what you believe as long as you're sincere." I'm here to tell you that it matters a great deal what you believe. It matters what you put in your soul just as it matters what you put in your stomach. You need to eat nutritious foods, but if we can agree on that, you have some "wiggle room" on what kinds of nutritious food you choose.

It's just like that with matters of faith. We know what is central, but there's a little room for us to personalize our faith.

By the way, you might wonder which End Times door I would enter. I have my own opinion, but I don't feel it's critical to convince you about why I believe it. Just call me "pan-millennial"—I believe it will all "pan out" just as God plans, and that's good enough for me.

I think there are people who obsess over some of these disputes. They think, "I can't wait until we all get to heaven, and I can show my buddy that I was right about the Second Coming, about predestination, about spiritual gifts" and on down the argument list. You know what's really going to happen? When you and I are in the presence of God, we'll have all the answers—and we won't even care. We will be in the presence of our wonderful Lord! Who's going to worry over the doctrinal details then?

Don't sweat the small stuff. If it won't matter then, why should it matter now?

Fighting Over Gifts

One of the most popular battlegrounds among Christians is the area of spiritual gifts. Think about it: these are *gifts*. God has given us something wonderful, and we turn it into a war. Have you ever seen little children surrounded by toys on Christmas morning, only to get caught up arguing with their siblings on how to play right? We do strange things sometimes.

Do you know what the purpose of gifts is? To serve the needs of others in the name of Christ. God's plan is for us to use the gifts of the Holy Spirit to build up the body of Christ and make it strong, vibrant, and healthy, so that together we can reach a lost world for Christ. Yet in too many instances we've allowed arguments about the gifts to foster disunity and confusion. Certain gifts are commonly understood to be active in today's church, but others, especially "sign" gifts, often have believers waging war against each other. I say, let's quit fighting about the Holy Spirit and his gifts! It's great that you're fully convinced in your own mind about which gifts are or are not active today, but that doesn't mean you can't respect others who see it differently. If necessary, agree to disagree with fellow believers on this issue, but for Christ's sake (and I mean that literally), don't allow your differences to create division. After all, we need each other.

And if you are proud of having certain gifts, please remember that God didn't give them to you to make you proud. The Bible doesn't support the notion of an elite group who use superior gifts. In fact, it does just the opposite. All spiritual gifts are given to glorify God, and if you use them to make others feel inferior, you're not obeying the Holy Spirit at all.

The gifts, when we use them right, make us something like an orchestra. You wouldn't really want to hear an orchestra made entirely of bassoons or entirely of oboes. But when there is diversity and balance in the instrumentation, and when everybody plays in harmony, the music is beautiful. The problems come when we start trying to ignore the sheet music and start soloing, or when we begin trying to drown out the strings or the percussion. It takes humility and discipline to play in an orchestra. The end product is one symphony. Nobody hears your bassoon or someone else's viola—they hear one melody that couldn't exist without all of you playing together. Do you think the clarinet player disdains the tuba, because the tuba is too deep? Do you think the violin player believes the timpani players should have a gentler, more flowing sound like she does? That would be silly, of course. The differences are more than allowable—they make the music possible as well as transcendent.

That's the way we should do things in the church. Let's say you're fully convinced about your particular belief system regarding eschatology. But you discover that certain other Bible believing Christians in your church or fellowship group don't share your view. Rather than start a feud, you can rejoice that the other interpretations fall within the pale of orthodoxy and that all of us agree on the essential point: Jesus is coming again!

Soon, all of us will know which school of thought has it right when it comes to eschatology. But in the meantime, humility and harmony are in order.

In fact, all of the disputes within the family of God will soon be resolved. We'll have all the answers. Or we'll be so awe-struck in the presence of our King that we'll have no memory of what the questions were or why we deemed them so important. We won't want to do anything but worship God and enjoy Him forever.

Parents: This Is for You

Do you get the general idea about picking our battles wisely? It has a great effect on how we live and love together as the church, but it's also a great issue in families. I hear from many parents who say, "I just don't understand my teenager. We raised her the very best way we knew how, took her to church, taught her all the right values, and now it seems like some kind of alien from another planet has taken over his life! We don't see eye to eye on anything, and the smallest matter becomes an all-out war with guns blazing and doors slamming."

Listen, I know where you're coming from. There are a lot of those teenagers from other planets roaming this earth. They text each other little messages that you and I can't even read, combinations of letters and numbers that may well be about taking over the world for all we know. Parents and older children have always had their challenges. That's nothing new. But the greatest problems come when we begin to look at parenting as an extended conflict instead of an adventure in training and growth.

You're going to have arguments and disagreements, and something's gotta give when that happens. You simply have to manage this season of family life. One of the most critical words of advice I can offer you is to choose your battles wisely. You can dig in your heels, use your parental power and win every single one of them, but you'll surely lose the "war" if you do that. You'll harm a loving relationship that is the work of your child's lifetime. On the other hand, if you surrender, throw up your hands, and say, "Have it your way—live however you want," you've then abandoned your God-given responsibility as a guide for your child's growth and development.

Instead, you have to look at the whole map. Find out where you can give ground and where you have to hold it. Or as the old country song said, you have to know when to hold 'em, and know when to fold 'em.

Let's say your teenage daughter is in the midst of making over her entire appearance. She is intending all kinds of body-piercing, tattoos, and hair colors not found in nature. There's no quicker way to hit a parent's panic button. What are you going to do?

a) Forbid your child from making any change at all. Tell her you'll be monitoring her wardrobe for appropriate choices, throwing out the hair dye, and forget all that other stuff.

b) Tell your child how much you'll be embarrassed in front of your friends. Whine a little about how disappointed you are in her choices. Then say, "It's your life. Go ahead and ruin yourself and disgrace the family."

c) Say, "Let's sit down and talk about it. I'd like to hear your plans and reasons for them." As you talk, you can explain why you have to draw a line with certain choices. Perhaps you can also find some places to make gentle concessions.

I'm not saying everybody's going to be 100 percent satisfied with the result of the negotiations. The important thing is that you're building a bridge rather than taking position behind walls and firing back and forth. You'll find that the more you talk together, the more love you show, the less your child will want to displease you. There's a kind of invisible account we have in our families. We accrue credit by giving ground to our children whenever we can do so as responsible parents. Your child asks for something, you're not crazy about allowing it, but you can live with it. Doing that on disputable matters makes it possible to draw the line on non-disputable ones. It's true in every place where people coexist.

Together at His Feet

Under the right circumstances, we could stop arguing and do what we need to do. I believe that, don't you?

Imagine you're having that summit meeting with your child about appearance issues. Suddenly the unthinkable happens. The house catches fire, or you receive some terrible news about a relative. In times of crisis, we seem to come together as a family. We discover that we can get together and support each other. It's just a matter of wanting to do so. It shouldn't take a tragedy or problem to create the bridge that we should be building ourselves, but it often happens that way.

Think about an occasion in recent American history. Hurricane Katrina hit the Gulf Coast in the southern United States in 2005. After that devastating tragedy, churches began to shine. They all lined up and worked side by side, shoulder to shoulder, with thousands of volunteers working to help the poor people who had lost everything they owned. If you had been there in New Orleans or on the beaches of Mississippi, you wouldn't have heard many arguments. You would have encountered pastors working together — Methodists, Baptists, Pentecostal, any brand you can name. Maybe Emo Philips' denomination, the Northern Conservative Fundamentalist Baptist, Great Lakes Region, Council of 1879, was there working right beside its blood rival from the other council. Who knows? People had no time to draw lines in the sand. Nobody thought to argue doctrine; people were simply too busy serving Jesus.

Should it require such a tragedy to force us to accept one another? Daily life may not seem as dramatic as the aftermath of Katrina, but we do have some challenges in this world. We have streets filled with people who don't know God, who are miserable, who are lonely, and who desperately need something that we have the potential of making available to them. Should we lose a single second getting hot and bothered over disputable matters?

I heard a story that is said to have happened in the 1960s, when someone first coined that term of "the Generation Gap." Kids had gone through some dramatic cultural changes, but the church was still holding fast to its stodgy old ways.

There was a conservative, affluent church across the street from a college campus. This church was really a cathedral, a formal place where everyone dressed up and sat quietly while the organ and the choir performed. Meanwhile, at the university, a young, longhaired male student had become curious about Christ. He had never been inside a church in his life, nor had he apparently taken a shower recently. On this Sunday morning, he loped across the street in his torn jeans and t-shirt, barefoot and smoking a cigarette. He walked into the narthex of the church, then into the sanctuary. Heads were quietly turning. There were more than a few cold stares. Everyone waited for an usher to show the rascal out. But apparently the ushers were somewhere putting away the beautiful, polished offering plates. The disturbance continued.

The student happily looked around the room, and then admired the high, arched ceiling. He began to walk down the aisle, and everyone took a collective deep breath as he proceeded all the way to the very front of the sanctuary. He hunkered down on the carpet just a few feet from the lectern.

At this point, there were audible gasps. Everyone was wondering what to do. Someone needed to take care of this crisis!

Someone did. From a pew near the back of the room, an elderly man stood up. He was wearing an expensive suit, a picture of dignity. He was probably in his seventies, surely not a match for a healthy young student who may put up a fight.

But the elderly man strolled calmly down the aisle and stopped next to the young student. With visible difficulty, he lowered himself to the floor and sat beside the student, who turned and gave him a big smile. The old man returned his smile. Both of them turned their gaze to the pastor, who hadn't spoken in several minutes, and worship resumed.

"What I'm about to preach," the minister began, "you'll never remember. What you've just seen, you'll never forget."

All the differences, all the petty things, fade away when we turn our eyes to true worship. Paul tells us that these three things abide: faith, hope and love. That final one, he says, is the greatest of all. It's so powerful it can make us forget to fight.

4.

Avoiding Arrogance: Seeing Ourselves Rightly

⌐⌐

I guess I'm showing my age. Those of you under 50 may not know what I'm talking about. The rest of you may smile a little bit.

When we were growing up, many of the saints had a list of things you could not do on the Lord's Day (Sunday). That was a different world, wasn't it? Nowadays there are youth soccer games on Sundays. Most stores and restaurants are open and doing a thriving business, with the admirable exception of the Chick-fil-A fast food franchise. Its owner is a churchgoing Christian from the old school, and he sacrifices all that after-church lunch business on Sunday by keeping his restaurants closed to honor God. For most of the rest of the world, however, Sunday is the new Saturday.

Yet when I was a youngster, it was generally understood in many Christian families that certain activities were off limits on the Lord's Day. I remember wondering what was up with that—if you could do them on Monday through Saturday, why not Sunday?

We hold to our faith all our lives, and therefore our practices develop a little residue that calcifies and becomes tradition. When Handel first wrote his choral masterpiece *The Messiah*, he conducted it before the king. That leader was so moved, so worshipful that he spontaneously stood in awe and praise when the strains of the Hallelujah Chorus rang out. Since he was the king, of course, everybody else immediately got on their feet. Today, hundreds of years later, audiences still stand for the Hallelujah Chorus, without a king in sight.

I think that's a good tradition. And for some people, avoiding certain activities on Sunday is important as well. But ultimately, our admission into heaven won't depend on whether we played cards or went to a movie on church day. It will rest on whether we accepted the gift of the death and resurrection of Jesus Christ, paying for our sins on the cross.

That's why the right or wrong answers about disputable matters are less important than the right or wrong behavior alongside them. Paul states it clearly in these two verses:

The man who eats everything must not look down on him who does not, and the man who does not eat everything must not condemn the man who does, for God has accepted him. Who are you to judge someone else's servant? To his own master he stands or falls. And he will stand, for the Lord is able to make him stand.

(Romans 14:3-4)

Remember our first-century situation? A couple of Christians go through the Wednesday night dinner line at church fellowship. They sit down at the long table with their trays, and one of them suddenly spots what's on the other's plate. It's a pork chop!

Nothing could be more shocking. For two hundred years before the time of Paul, many Jews actually died for refusing to eat pork. The Greeks had a real taste for barbecue and couldn't understand this attitude. This was a new world of Greek culture and Roman travel, and most people were easing up on their quaint old sacred traditions, particularly where the lunch menu was involved. But the Hebrew people believed that Moses had provided some pretty permanent rules when he came down from that mountain. Dietary restrictions were serious business, and most Jews continued to follow them wherever they traveled in the Mediterranean world.

Our first fellow is one of those traditionalists. And just as he is gasping over the evil pork chop looming before him, another friend sits down on his other side. This one, thankfully, has a big, juicy cheeseburger on his plate with an order of onion rings. He has checked his biblical concordance and there's nothing in there about cheeseburgers. Beef is stamped heaven-approved. Just as he is about to let out a sigh of relief, however, he catches one other detail. His friend removes the burger from its paper wrapper, and the paper says, "Bob's Pagan Temple of South Rome: Over a Billion Idols Served."

Unbelievable! This hamburger patty came from meat sacrificed to an idol, one of God's competitors!

Enough is enough. The first fellow puts his entrée, his tea, and his cheesecake back on the tray and goes in search of more suitable dining companions. He mutters to himself, "The church is going to hell in a hand-basket. What was good for Moses, David, and Solomon is no longer good enough for these so-called Christians. Give me that old-time religion, breakfast, lunch, dinner, and snacks."

The pork chop and cheeseburger devotees look at each other, shake their heads, and roll their eyes dismissively. "Get a load of that guy, too good to eat with the likes of us. What a legalist! Food restrictions are *so* 50 BC. Somebody wake him up and tell him it's AD now!"

So the question is, who is in the right, and who is in the wrong? Paul's point is that both parties are asking the wrong question in the first place.

He establishes that technically, it's up to the individual's personal discretion to eat what he deems appropriate and tasty. The old Hebrew structure of law no longer has its hold on us. But that doesn't mean the pork and sacrifice eaters are "right," and the other guy is "wrong." The much more important question is how we deal with each other. In our illustration, both sides are guilty of a certain arrogance. The first man is haughty about traditions, and he makes them a barrier to fellowship with those who aren't connected to the same traditions. The other two men are haughty about their freedom. They won't stop to look at it from the other guy's perspective, and see why those longstanding traditions would hold tremendous emotional power for a longstanding Jew.

On the technical religious issue, both are right—for whatever little practical value that has. On the more important area of attitude, both are very wrong. And that has very significant practical consequences. Arrogance will destroy everything we try to do as Christians.

Break It Down

The humorist Garrison Keillor tells stories from Lake Wobegon, a fictional version of his own hometown in Minnesota. In his novel *Lake Wobegon Days*, he describes growing up in a Christian sect known as the Sanctified Brethren, "so tiny that nobody but us and God knew about it."

Keillor explains that his particular folks were "exclusive" brethren, "a branch that believed in keeping itself pure of false doctrine by avoiding association with the impure." Brethren who lived in the big cities and associated with "strangers" were known as "the so-called Open Brethren."

The stricter variety made sure that every tiny detail of the faith was agreed upon before any friendliness could be exchanged.

The Brethren had begun in England when about twenty families broke off from the Anglican Church over some burning question of correct worship. However, as Keillor writes,

Once having tasted the pleasure of being Correct and defending True Doctrine, they kept right on and broke up at every opportunity until, by the time I came along, there were dozens of tiny Brethren groups, none of which were speaking to any of the others.

Keillor explains that he grew up with church in the living room, and only a few approved participants. He is a humorist, and this is satire—but he hits a little too close to home, doesn't he? Our faith continues to spawn its spin-offs of denominations.

Then there's C. S. Lewis, the British author, who wrote a fantasy book called *The Great Divorce*. His title is a little misleading. It's really a story about a trip to heaven and a sideways glance at hell. He doesn't see the latter as a big chamber of fire and nasty demons, but a wilderness filled with lonely mansions. Everyone can have what he wants, but he never enjoys it because he can't get along with any other resident. Everyone lives alone, building more walls, pushing their residence ever farther apart from everyone else. That's a pretty good picture of hell, isn't it? A place with no bridges, but plenty of canyons; a place of miserable solitude.

That's what arrogance can do, my friend. It takes our pride and uses it as a stick to push us away from each other. Paul's operative phrase is this: *Learn not to look down.* "The man who does not (insert issue of the day) must not condemn the man who does, for God has accepted him." Know what you believe, work all that out carefully, and be confident in it in your own mind. Then allow others to come to their own conclusions, and honor whatever those conclusions may be.

Here's the reason, according to Paul:

God has accepted him. Who are you to judge someone else's servant? To his own master he stands or falls.

Remember, Paul sees every Christian as a "servant" of Christ. The real meaning, in that time, was slave. But let's understand what Paul meant when he called himself a slave or servant of Christ, and called us fellow slaves. He uses a Greek word that refers to a "bond-slave," and Moses explains all that in the books of Leviticus and Deuteronomy—the same scrolls they pulled off the shelf when they were arguing about holy holidays and "soul" food.

These slaves were simply people who had fallen into debt and could only work off the money by selling their sweat as farm workers. Yet Moses said that the owner should set them free on the seventh year, even if they still had a balance on the ledger, in honor of God setting their forefathers free when they were slaves in Egypt. Then, Moses said (and it often happened), the servant would have grown attached to the family, because he was treated with love as a family member anyway. He would ask to stay, and the owner would poke a tool called an awl through his earlobe and pronounce him a servant for life. There was no indignity to this at all, just a reflection of love and grace that is greater than the debt between two men.

Can you begin to see why Peter, Paul, James and others began referring to themselves (and us) as "bond-servants of Christ"? We were like that poor fellow who owed a monster lottery debt and had no hope of paying it off. Being set completely free, with his bill marked "paid in full," he would look up at the creditor and say, "I want to hang out with this guy from now on, if he will let me."

Servant to Servant

Christ has set us free. He is the very one appointed to sit in judgment one day, and he has already paid with his own blood, his own pain, his own full estrangement from God while on the cross, so that we could go free! If he could hang up for us, shouldn't we want to hang out with him? If he had his hands and feet pierced for us, can't we get our ears pierced for him? There should be a hole in your soul in the shape of a cross. Therefore, when we talk about being a "slave" of Christ, we miss what these first century Christians intended when they used that Greek word *doulos*, meaning someone who made himself a slave through his own debt, then chose in the joy of his freedom to continue to serve a loving master.

Now that you know that, look again at Romans 14:

God has accepted him. Who are you to judge someone else's servant? To his own master he stands or falls.

When you get into a pitched battle with your brother or sister over some disputable matter, you need to step back and realize what you're messing with. That person has chosen God, and God has pierced him and claimed him. The smaller details are between them, so why are you setting yourself up as a master of some kind? If that person is wrong, he will personally answer to his true master on that point. What's it to you, buddy?

That's the problem today. Most of us don't understand the true lines of authority in this world. You are accountable to God, and so is that other person. We want to set ourselves up as masters at church, at work, in marriage, or anywhere else. Then we want to impose our particular opinions upon the world, create replicas of ourselves in everyone we know. It's great to have all the answers, or to think we do. The Bible doesn't sanction know-it-alls, but it does tell us to be fully persuaded in our own minds about every issue. Our problem comes when we confuse our personal persuasion with social authority.

I've known people who met the Lord after being a slave to fashion. In their former life, they had all the designer clothing, and looking sharp was right at the top of their list of priorities. Then, as they stood at the foot of the cross and saw Jesus naked, whipped, and dying as the soldiers played poker over all that he owned, which was a simple robe— well, that changed my friends' attitude toward clothing, jewelry, and cosmetics. They felt called to tone it down a good bit, and they simplified their appearance and lifestyle. I've understood and approved. God knows exactly who we are and how we think. He finds that exact spot where we as individuals need to learn a crucial lesson, and he applies his discipline with wisdom and love to that place.

But what if that person, having gotten the message, then decided it was a matter for everyone? What if he or she decided to write a book about it, pull out all the right Bible verses, and start a crusade calling upon every single Christian to dress in peasant style? I've seen it happen, and you can imagine just how well it goes over in the typical church—it starts an uproar, and both sides are pulling out Bible verses and using them as ammunition. One side presents the splendor of Solomon, and the other quotes Jesus when he said that Solomon in all his splendor was no match for a simple lily. Never mind that fashion is not the focus in either of those Bible passages. Once the firing commences, this thing is no longer about humbly exploring God's Word, but about knocking the other person off his or her pedestal.

A Perennial Disputable Matter

One of the big issues in my youth was alcohol. Christ and cocktails were not mentioned in the same sentence. If you were saved, there was no question that you were never going to sip any form of intoxicant for the rest of your days, no exceptions. If you were at a wedding and the champagne was poured, you made a big point of refusing it or you knew the consequences as soon as you got back to church.

Is this a question every Christian must consider? Absolutely, now and always. Is it a disputable matter, an issue upon which we should give ground? Absolutely, now and always. Let people work it out with God themselves, as long as, for example, we don't see them becoming slaves to drinking, or compromising our testimony as ambassadors for Christ.

Those are different issues, of course. Sobriety and moderation are clear commands of Scripture. If your friend has a problem with alcohol and invites Christ into his life, he is saved—not after he gives up the bottle, but right now, right at the critical moment when he says yes to Jesus. But make no mistake; the Holy Spirit will lead him toward working on his particular weak spots, just as he did with the slave to fashion. We don't have to "clean up the house" before inviting Christ to wash us white as snow, but once he's there we'll see just how grimy everything is, and we'll want it to sparkle. And God will call other people to pitch in and help us tidy up. There are ministries in our church and elsewhere that allow people to work on such areas of personal challenge—drinking, drugs, every problem you can name. But we do it through friendship instead of force.

In my case, growing up in a spiritual culture that severely frowned upon alcohol, I was in for quite a lesson. I had picked up the perception that drinking was a sure sign of a "worldly" person, someone not committed to a life of faith. That's just how it worked, or so I'd been taught. I'll never forget the first time I was invited to dinner with some Christian friends. We had just been in a church setting in which I saw these people minister, and there was no question about their commitment. God was using these people. Then, at dinner, they ordered a glass of wine with their meal. My personal conviction was to avoid drinking in any circumstance, and I was persuaded in my own mind about that, to put it the way Paul does. But here were people who could use alcohol—at least a glass of wine—without being enslaved to it. You may laugh about my simplistic view of the world, but I wasn't laughing. I was thinking: "I thought these guys were saved!" They were. They were saved drinking a glass of wine while I was saved drinking a can of Pepsi.

I try to be involved in disciple building. I work with young men to get them started in the basics of the faith. We meet, study the Bible, pray together, and I encourage them in whatever challenges they're facing. My counsel to them is, "Brother, simply be alcohol-free." Don't even fool around with wine coolers, I urge, but steer clear of the whole business. It's common sense to me, because we know that alcohol can be slow and subtle in the way it ultimately destroys a life—and it can hamper someone's testimony based on the logic I was originally taught. So why not just punt on this whole issue? You won't miss that buzz; I know I never do.

That's my personal counsel but not my command. I'm serious when I instruct young men to read the Bible, to pray, to live out their faith. On certain other things, I simply try to give good advice. That's one of them.

The H-Word

The church is full of hypocrites! Recognize that hit tune?

It's one of the classic excuses for staying away from the church: "It's too full of hypocrites." The right answer is, "Of course it is, and we can always use another one." We're not perfect, just saved and working on it.

All the same, we want to avoid hypocrisy whenever we can. Anyone who sets himself up to live to a high standard, spiritual or otherwise, must guard against the appearance of hypocrisy. This is another reason to avoid the arrogance we're discussing in this chapter. Arrogance is a gateway attitude to hypocrisy.

Here's how it works. Pick your pet issue and take your hard line. Let's say it's drinking. Real Christians, you say, never touch a drop. Once you take that position, you'd better be consistent in every area of life, because you can bet that people will be searching your life for inconsistencies, with a fine toothcomb. Let's say you're expounding on the evil of alcohol, and then you tell me you can't start the day without a cup of coffee. I'm going to notice a disconnect there. You're talking about wine or whiskey as a stimulant that can be habit-forming, but you make that trip to Starbucks for the tall cup every day? Can't that be a drinking problem, too?

"Oh, that's different," you say. "You can't get drunk on coffee." Wired, perhaps, but not intoxicated. Still, doesn't perception come in here somewhere? Don't we tell people (as I've just admitted doing) that it's a matter of creating a stumbling block in your witness to others? If so, think twice about telling me you can't start the day without a cup of fully-caffeinated java.

This may be a brand new thought for you, because hardly anyone in church makes an issue out of coffee-drinking, nor should they, really. By the same token, we tend to look unfavorably upon the cigarette smoker. By this time, I wouldn't be the only person encouraging younger people to simply steer clear—be smoke-free. The body is the temple of the Holy Spirit, and smoking a lot of cigarettes over time is like going into the temple with a sledgehammer and pounding away at the columns. Why would anyone want to do that to the temple of God?

Yet there are Christians who still struggle with smoking. It's incredibly difficult to beat that habit. If you haven't had to do it yourself, it won't do for you to make this issue a battlefield, to contemptuously tell your smoker friend that it's a "cancer stick" and so on. Your friend is thinking, "You have no idea what this is like. If you think it's so easy to stop, you're living in fantasy land." And you've just built a wall rather than a bridge. Going back to C. S. Lewis's admonition, what tempts me may not be the thing that tempts you. It's easy for us to declare victory over the giants we never have to face. But as long as there is some area where you struggle, some giant on your horizon, you need to show mercy or stand accused of hypocrisy.

I can remember a time years ago when I was an assistant pastor. I recognized a man from our church at the corner, and I saw him puffing away at a cigarette. He saw me coming, and he knew that people at our church disapproved of smoking. It was on our unspoken Top Ten list of forbidden things. I rolled down my window and greeted him: "Hey, man, how's it going?"

In a Christian world that was working right, he could have said, "Well, you see what I'm doing here. I'm a little embarrassed, but I wish you would pray for me. I need victory in my life over this habit." We could have prayed together and I hope I could have helped him.

Instead, in the culture we've created in our churches, he felt the desperate need to hide his problem rather than share it. He whisked the cigarette behind his back in a rather awkward way. I knew it, he knew I knew it, and both of us felt uncomfortable. I wondered if he was burning the back of his coat, but the truth is, there was a burning need for honesty at that moment.

The O-Word

That's not how we're supposed to live together as brothers and sisters in Christ, my friend. The struggler shouldn't be conditioned to expect judgment, and the rest of us shouldn't be on the lookout for things to criticize. It should work more like James laid it out in the New Testament: "Therefore confess your sins to each other and pray for each other so that you may be healed. The prayer of a righteous man is powerful and effective" (James 5:16). The condemnation of a self-righteous man is powerful and destructive.

To raise another uncomfortable example, let's invoke the O-word: *Overeating.* That one's not on many Top Ten lists, but if you're going to criticize the other guy's temple, you'd better keep an eye on your own bay window. Strangely enough, here's another "weighty issue" where the church hasn't taken much of a stand over the years. There are usually a few deacons or elders who are more than weighting down their end of the pew. The pastor himself is often someone who would benefit from a low-cal diet. But if it's wrong to damage the temple of the human body through cigarettes or whiskey, is it any less wrong to do so by calories or caffeine?

It seems pretty obvious when we lay out the issue, but that doesn't stop people from being inconsistent, does it? If we're going to tackle the issues, we'd better tackle all of them. And we'd also better start with the man or woman in the mirror. We've already made reference to what Jesus said about this: Don't go after the speck in someone else's eye until that massive beam is no longer obstructing your own. And the way that principle would work out, if we ever lived by it, would be that we'd find ourselves very quiet and respectful of others. That wouldn't be such a bad idea. If we were careful to steer clear of hypocrisy, we would learn not to be arrogant.

Over the years I've seen a lot of people in a panic to hide who they really were. I walk up to the door, someone looks out the window, and I hear the muffled voices: "Here comes the pastor! Put that stuff away!" I hear the bottles being pushed into a cabinet, air freshener blanketing the tobacco aroma, whatever. I'm used to it. I simply walk a little slower, act like I'm taking my time, enjoying the garden; I know they're busy putting on their masks. But I want to say, "Hey, just leave everything the way it is. Leave it all out on the table, whatever. I've come to encourage you and minister to you, certainly not condemn you." Unfortunately, people often expect arrogance in Christian leaders.

But why? Who exactly is the model, the trend-setter that makes everyone expect us to be critical and judgmental? It's supposed to be Jesus, who had not an ounce of arrogance or unkindness within him; Jesus, who sought out the flamboyant sinners in every town and invited himself to their homes. People couldn't believe he associated with tax collectors, women of ill repute, drunkards, pretty much the usual suspects from the Top Ten list.

That's why so many people who met him followed him right out of town. He just kept collecting followers, people who wanted to be his bond-servant. He released them from disease, from confusion, from self-condemnation, and from every sin you can imagine, but they didn't want to be released from *him*.

Philippians 2:5 commands us to have that same attitude as the one we find in the mind of Christ. He himself was God, but chose not to clutch at that and hold it over others. Instead, he humbled himself for the benefit of others. That is precisely the opposite of arrogance. That is the complete disavowal of hypocrisy. It's the willingness to go all the way to the cross for people, to love them for who they are rather condemn them for not being us.

Someone Else's Job

There's at least one other good reason for avoiding the arrogance of judging each other on disputable matters. The truth is that when you judge your friend's behavior, you're encroaching on someone else's job—and messing up the perfect way he does it.

Who is this mysterious person whose job it is to point out people's failings? If you're a Christian, you know him pretty well, though you may not choose to pay attention to his advice as often as you should. He became your best friend the day you became a believer. He is willing to go anywhere you need to go, and there's nothing in the world he won't talk about with you. He's the most positive and encouraging person you'll ever be fortunate enough to know, and though he will indeed point out what's wrong in your life, he won't beat you up over it or let you beat yourself up. He's gentle, compassionate, and constructive. He's also generous, having already given you at least one incredible gift that you can use every day of your life.

You've guessed that I'm talking about the Holy Spirit, the intimate presence of God himself in our lives; the still, small voice who whispers words of encouragement and conviction to our souls. He works with your friends so you won't have to. It's his job to point out those areas that need to be turned over to him for transformation. In the fourteenth chapter of John, Jesus said he would send this comforter, the Holy Spirit, to abide with us forever. He said it was better for him, Jesus, to leave so that the Spirit could come—that's how wonderful it is to have the Spirit of God living within us.

He never condemns, but gently and helpfully convicts. Sometimes you feel it, you "hear" that voice, just after you say sharp words to someone. You think, "Why did I say that? God wouldn't want me to be like this." Where does that sudden impression come from? Our intuition tells us that it's not self-generated. If it were, we'd be harder on ourselves, just as we've learned from others. But the Spirit's voice is accurate, gentle, encouraging, mildly rebuking. You can never help your friend the way the Holy Spirit can. If you're sure the friend should share your opinion about it, you talk to the Holy Spirit yourself and leave it up to him. He's got a good track record for doing the right thing by others.

And What About You?

Let's make one other observation about the Spirit's place in this issue of correction. I know that as you've read this chapter, you've thought about those times when you've had an arrogant attitude toward others. But you've also thought about your own issues where you might be the one who is criticized. Maybe it has to do with overeating or with some area that you know is keeping you from all that God wants you to be.

I want you to know that when you're severely critical of yourself, that's not the voice of God. He is the only one who can discipline us with perfect love. It may hurt sometimes, because we know we've done wrong and we feel the regret. But the touch of the Spirit on our soul encourages us to repent, which means to turn around and go the other way. He encourages us to get the victory in life. Every time you or I hear and heed that voice, we become a little more like the image of Christ toward which we are slowly being transformed.

No matter how far you advance toward looking and living like Christ, you'll still have those off-days. We all do. The Bible says not to walk in the flesh, but to walk in the Spirit. Yet we have those days when we walk in the flesh anyway. As you grow more mature, you'll be better at hearing his voice saying, "This is not a plan." You'll freely allow him to deal with you and get it straight, and you'll feel one step closer to the amazing creation he is making you to be, his workmanship, created to do good works.

Don't you wish we could be that way with each other— as gentle and loving and transformational as the Holy Spirit is with us? Don't worry, because again, this is the Holy Spirit's job, the inner coach who does it perfectly. Your job is simply to be you, to help people rather than judging them, to love them rather than trying to make them be just like you. Be assured in your own mind of your beliefs, but be humble enough about them to accept the way others feel. Be conscious of your own weaknesses, of the fact that you don't have all the answers. But love yourself, forgive yourself, and refuse to condemn yourself, because God, in all his perfection, loves and forgives you. Every flaw you have has already been covered, already been washed by the blood of Christ.

Therefore, I encourage you to get out your Top Ten list of disputable issues and say goodbye to it. You know where you stand on them, so in the case of others, leave it to God. Say goodbye to arrogance and hypocrisy. Love others with all that you are, knowing that the world will know you are Christ's disciple because you love people the way Christ does. And once you've done these things, you will feel free as you haven't felt free in many years; free of the massive burden of others' righteousness. Isn't it great not to have to be in charge of everyone else you know and how they live?

It's great to be set free, isn't it?

5.

Avoiding Assumptions: Getting Over Our Preconceptions

M y preacher friend was holding a revival at a church out of town. He really got into his preaching, and the congregational response was amazing. Everyone was getting excited. My friend noticed a little man sitting on the second row who was leaning forward the whole time, as if he had something very important to say.

At the end of the sermon, the preacher invited people to come forward if they had any kind of special prayer needs. There was an immediate stream of people flowing down the center aisle, needing prayers for their health, their marriage, their job situations, and everything else you can imagine. My friend noticed the little man in the crowd, but people kept shoving past him. Preacher felt a real burden for this fellow by now, and he made his way over to him, kind of leaned over toward him and asked, "How can I minister to you today?"

The little man said, "I was wondering if you'd pray for my hearing."

Preacher immediately felt great compassion for the man. He grabbed him and pulled him forward in a tight embrace, and began to call out to the Lord to heal this man's problem. He laid a hand on the little man's bald head, the other hand on his right ear, continued his prayer, and finally put his mouth right up to the ear and shouted right into it: "Brother, how is your hearing now?"

The little man replied, "I don't know, it's not scheduled until next week."

All right, I'll admit to you that this story never happened, as far as I know. But I would venture that something like it happens every day somewhere, because we make assumptions just a little too quickly. If you're anything like most people, you meet someone and get a quick read on who they are. You have a collection of previously prepared labels, and in your mind, you quickly and efficiently slap the right label on a new acquaintance. More often than not, of course, you later have to go back into your mental files and pry that label right off. Most of us aren't nearly as good at quick judgments as we think we are. But we all make assumptions and presumptions, and they're always based on our previous experience and current agenda. The preacher was all set up to understand one thing when he heard the little man's words, but what he "understood" was not what the man was trying to communicate. And he ended up embarrassing both of them.

This book is about building a bridge to other people, and getting over it. One of the hardest parts of that bridge to get over is the tendency toward personal preconception. It's really a subtle form of the arrogance that we discussed in the last chapter—the arrogance that comes when we begin to behave as if everyone should see things exactly as we do.

Have you ever been at a party or gathering when the subject of politics came up, and everyone seemed to share the same perspective except you? Perhaps it was a group of Christians or a group from your workplace. People often assume that because they are already in some kind of grouping, that everyone else must share their views on everything. It feels awkward. You nod and smile politely, if you're not the confronting type, and you hope the subject will drift in some other direction pretty soon. I know that non-believers feel it when a little circle of people assumes everyone in the group goes to church on Sunday and believes in the same kind of God. Christians themselves feel that way when the shoe is on the other foot.

This is just an ordinary and uncomfortable part of life, isn't it? We want to walk happily through life along bridges of friendship that connect us to everyone we meet. Yet these little moments of false assumption underline the things we don't share, the bridges that are not built. That's why we need to think, in this chapter, about the tendency to presume.

Sleep, Creep, Leap!

We lose the sensitivity and consideration that would keep the awkward moments from happening because arrogance usually creeps in very stealthily. It's like the kudzu, that ivy found along highways in the Deep South that originally came from Asia. It has just about taken over some of those states, covering whole forests and hills, climbing the walls of houses and snaking across the roofs. They say that when kudzu is put into the soil, the first year it sleeps; the second year it creeps; the third year it leaps!

So much of what we Christians call sin is just like that, isn't it? If you ever gained a lot of weight, the situation kind of crept up on you, didn't it? Even at those times when you had an explosive argument with someone, maybe you figured out later that the emotions that fueled it crept on you over a long period of time.

Arrogance "creeps," too. It was out topic for the last chapter, and we're going to stay with it here. But this time we're going to talk about a subtle aspect of the arrogance that divides us from others. I'm talking about how we come to believe some of the things we do in life and particularly at church, and how we slowly begin to presume that our opinions are the final authority.

We've been looking at Paul's advice to the Romans about these issues. As Romans 14 continues, he is still addressing the issue of disagreements over whether to celebrate special days or eat certain kinds of food:

> *He who regards one day as special, does so to the Lord. He who eats meat, eats to the Lord, for he gives thanks to God; and he who abstains, does so to the Lord and gives thanks to God. For none of us lives to himself alone and none of us dies to himself alone. If we live, we live to the Lord; and if we die, we die to the Lord. So, whether we live or die, we belong to the Lord.*
>
> *For this very reason, Christ died and returned to life so that he might be the Lord of both the dead and the living. You, then, why do you judge your brother? Or why do you look down on your brother? For we will all stand before God's judgment seat. It is written:*
> *"As surely as I live,' says the Lord,*
> *'every knee will bow before me;*
> *every tongue will confess to God.'"*
> *So then, each of us will give an account of himself to God.*
>
> (Romans 14:6-12)

As we've seen, Paul is hammering away at this issue of who's the boss. He does it with the phrase "to the Lord." You ultimately make eating decisions to the Lord. You ultimately assign your celebrations to the Lord. In the long run, he says, you will live and die completely to the Lord. What is he talking about? God is the boss. Remember, we are bond-servants of Christ. We have chosen to live in his household, even as he has set us free, because we know that no one will love us better. Our deepest joy is the servitude of living for him.

But just because we've chosen to come back to that household of the Master on our own free will, we haven't gained the right to boss the other servants around. Important distinction: He has made me free, but he has not made me the boss of you. He retains that distinction. This is Paul's great point throughout the fourteenth chapter of Romans. Every one of us must decide before God how to live our lives. As he says in our final verse above, each one will stand before God and give an account of himself or herself—but not for anyone else. Not your spouse; not your child; not your best buddy.

Therefore when we try to call the shots for others, when we hand them position papers on what they're going to believe or do, we ruin the beauty of the fellowship he is building.

WWJD?

We all remember the WWJD fad that hit the Christian world years ago. The initials stood for What Would Jesus Do? That was an inspired idea, particularly for teenagers. They wore a little bracelet with those four letters and got a little reminder to think about the practical example of Jesus Christ as they went about their daily lives.

But in so many situations, how do we know what Jesus would do? The answer is not always so clear. We're going to look at a few more issues in which you might decide Jesus would take one course, while I might decide it would be the opposite direction. Both of us, mind you, are sincere Christians. Both of us pray and read the Bible. But there are many life issues that cut just a little too fine to pull a definitive answer from the Scriptures.

WWJD is a helpful paradigm particularly for the new Christian. The young believer comes along and finds someone who has a simple need, perhaps can't afford the next meal, and he thinks, "What would Jesus do?" Well, the answer there is pretty much a no-brainer: If Jesus had the money, he'd buy him a meal. No problem there.

But then the new Christian is invited to go to a particular kind of party where he knows a lot of questionable activities will be occurring, and he asks, "What would Jesus do?" The fact is that right there in the New Testament we read about Jesus going to parties and hanging out with questionable people with loose lifestyles. So he thinks, "Jesus hung out with a lot of sinners, so I will, too!"

You see the problem: Jesus was the Son of God. He had the wisdom and spiritual authority to deal with any situation that might arise. He had withstood the direct temptation of the devil in the wilderness, so he could handle a rough party. But what about a young Christian?

In that situation, strangely enough, even if Jesus or some hero of the Bible would do it, that doesn't necessarily mean we should. There was a sad story in the newspaper recently about a man in the city of Kiev who went to the zoo and jumped into a pit where wild lions were on display. As he did so, he shouted, "If God exists, he will save me!" Maybe he was following the model of Daniel, who was *placed*—note: did not jump—into the lions' den. Tragically, no miracle happened. A lioness immediately pounced upon the man and ripped into him, killing him instantly. It was a sad way to make the point that when we make a proclamation about the will of God on some matter, we had better know we can back it up. The zoo victim was presumptuous. He made an assumption about what God would do in such a situation, and he paid for it with his life.

The problem is that we're tempted to misuse the Word of God to justify and further our own agenda. We have a record of what he, Moses, David, Paul, and many other models did, and it's too easy to twist those stories and teachings into a shape that serves our purposes.

Have you ever noticed that some people are morning people by natural constitution, while others just hate the early hours and get more done after the sun has set? Morning Christians tend to remind you that Jesus once left early in the morning to spend time alone with God. Therefore, they point out, everyone should have their devotional time in the morning, based on that one Scriptural citation.

Well, you couldn't lose by doing that. We all need to spend time with God on a daily basis, and morning is a handy time—the day is all out in front of us. But can we be certain that on that particular day in his life, Jesus was trying to establish a once-for-all-time dictate on the approved time of day for prayer and devotions? I'm not sure about that. Maybe you're a night person, and you're simply able to connect with God better before you go to bed. That time has its advantages, too. This is just a little thing, I agree, but just another subtle example of spiritual presumption. You take your daily prayer time to the Lord, and I take mine to the Lord. We need to be fully convinced in our own minds of how to live, then it's between God and each of us.

Now keep in mind that you can offer your friends a story on what's helped for you. You can say, "If you're like me, you'll find that morning is a great time for devotions. Here are some of the things I like about it." You just can't be pushy. So much of what causes problems among us is not the content so much as the presentation.

Presumption About Worship

In church, one of the great battlefields is the subject of worship. It's amazing just how controversial this area has been during the last couple of decades. As I said earlier, there was a season of relative peace on this particular topic. Oh, there was "high church" music in one kind of setting, gospel tunes in another, and even a few folk masses with guitar-strumming here and there. But for the most part, it seemed as if everyone knew the rules, and felt that the "right" kind of worship culture could be found at the exact kind of church he or she already chose.

But in recent years, things began to change. People wanted to mix things up a little bit, bring new sounds into old venues. I can remember the early 1970s when my bunch began to encounter a fresh new kind of music by names like André Crouch and the Disciples, Edwin Hawkins, and others. The whole idea of music for God that sounded fresh enough to be on the mainstream radio stations—we were excited! We wanted to be a part of that as soon as possible.

We went to the pastor and told him we wanted to start a youth choir. Naturally, he thought that was a great idea, and he was happy to see our enthusiasm. We said, "We want it to be like these records," and we gave him some of our LPs. He agreed to listen to them, and he heard that the music lifted up Jesus even though it wasn't conventional church music by recent standards.

We said, "We want to do this right, and that means having drums and electric guitar and electric bass in the sanctuary."

The pastor looked thoughtful and told us he wanted to help us with that. "We might be able to do this," he said, "but we need to show our respect to some of the saints in our congregation. You have to understand they're just not used to the idea of drums and things like that."

And he did that, gently and respectfully. One of those older saints was my dad's mother, and she was one of these people who had "saint" written all over her. You've probably known one. You could just look at her and know that she went to church and lived her faith the rest of the time. I'll never forget her coming to question me about this music idea. She looked a little dubious to say the least; her eyes were squinted speculatively and her mouth and nose were drawn up. "So you and your friends are starting a young people's choir?"

I told my grandmother that's exactly what we were doing.

She said, "You're going to bring drums into the church?"

"Yes ma'am," I said. "We hope to. It's music about Jesus, and it's the kind of music that will help get kids my age into a worship service."

She nodded and went back for more perspective from the pastor, who just happened to be her son. He explained that these songs honored the Lord, but they did it in a language that younger people could hear and understand.

When we had our big debut in the worship service, my grandmother sat in her pew and listened carefully. I stole a peek at her once or twice, a little worried about whether she would leave, hold her ears, just vanish in a little explosion, or what. At the end of the service, she walked right up to our drummer. "Young man," she said, in that voice that, like her face, told the world she was a saint and attention must be paid.

"Yes ma'am?" asked our drummer with saucer-sized eyes.

"I wasn't too happy when I heard they were going to let you bring drums into our church. But I came, and I listened, and I found myself tapping my foot a little."

We all smiled.

"I found myself really caught up in the music," she said. "I have to admit, I enjoyed it. I also enjoyed the way you didn't bang those drums too loud."

We heaved sighs of relief. Message received: As long as we didn't make her ears vibrate or break the glass in her spectacles, our two sides could get along.

You know what? A small bridge was crossed at that moment. Drums didn't fit into my grandmother's spiritual world at the time, but she built a bridge and got over it. When she walked up to talk to our drummer, she was crossing that bridge because it was important that we see her do it. There may have been other saints who were afraid to make the short journey, to connect with us young renegades, but in time, we made it through this period of musical transition. We were able to reach a lot of people in my generation who are now serving the Lord, and perhaps would be doing something else otherwise.

Worship: The Next Generation

Even so, I attend pastors conferences were, even to this day, where there are leaders who rail against "loud" worship. "The Lord is in his holy temple," they quote. "Let all the earth keep silent before him." Yet is it fair to use that Bible verse? Didn't David lead the children of Israel in worshipful dancing? Don't we have psalms about breaking out all the musical instruments? Doesn't Psalm 100 tell us to "make a joyful noise?"

Well, that's my perspective but it's still up to me to love and respect my pastoral brother who interprets the theology of worship differently. We might even have to build that bridge back the other way, because time can play a joke on us by turning us into the "older saints" who are dismissive of the other side. The bridge always has two sides.

And sometimes it needs to be extended a little farther out in the same direction. Now we have good folks who want to make the music "louder." André Crouch wouldn't cause a stir in many churches by this time, but the debate has shifted to hip-hop, rap, and Christian rock as expressions of worship. The kind of people who were in our youth choir are now being challenged by some of the newer sounds, and what we must do is give these kids the same grace that was given to us. My grandmother set a model for me; she was convinced in her mind about a disputable matter, but she didn't try to make a universal restriction out of it.

Sometimes an out-of-culture experience can help us get the perspective we need. I was talking to a friend about these things, about the difference in one church's range of worship expression and another's. He asked me, "Do you know where I had the most powerful experience in worship I've ever had?"

I was interested in hearing him answer his own question. We usually assume that our own most powerful worship would be in a setting that is precisely to our personal cultural taste in music, preaching, and so on.

My friend said, "My most intense experience came on a visit to Africa. I saw myself going over there as a blessed, fortunate American who had it all. I figured that out of the goodness of my heart, I was sharing a few crumbs of our American greatness with these folks in Africa."

He continued, "Well, I was turned upside down. What I encountered was people walking several hours to worship in this village—then standing on their feet for a few more hours to praise God. We wise, blessed, Americans might sit in a pew and keep an eye on the clock and the cell phone, eager to get out to the restaurant buffet. These folks were absolutely focused and intent upon lifting up the name of Jesus, and nothing else. They lifted their voices and it lifted my spirit, so that I was caught up in worship myself. Their music was powerful, anointed. It had nothing to do with the presence or absence of organs, pianos, drums, electric or acoustic guitars, anything plugged or unplugged. It was all about who they were and how they laid it at the feet of God. The Spirit of the Lord was enthroned on their praises—you could feel it!"

He was quiet for a moment, then said, "And there I was, having crossed the ocean to teach them how to connect with God. Instead, He sent me over so they could teach me. What a humbling experience—what a worshipful experience."

You see, no matter where you stand, you're on one side of a bridge. You probably perceive yourself to be on some kind of a mountain peak, a pinnacle of wisdom higher than others. But the ground is level, and we all stand on some side of a bridge—and at the other end lies something to be learned, something that will enrich our encounter with God.

Before we leave this topic of what is right for worship, here's what I think from my side of the bridge right now. We need to keep finding new ways to exalt the Lord. At any given time, we do a pretty good job with one particular way—but we can get too married to that approach. A lot of churches today do a great job with praise; they have praise bands that can really enhance the beauty of a song. We're no longer afraid of a little noise in the sanctuary. But maybe praise is only one side of worship. Maybe we do need to let the earth keep silent every now and then, and find God in the quiet. We can read the Psalms, or we can worship without music. We just need to keep finding fresh ways to experience the Lord rather than simply be culturally comfortable. Don't assume or presume to have a monopoly on worship through how you're doing it this week.

Building bridges is all about the fresh experience.

$$$

Wealth vs. poverty: As you can see, I'm intent on pushing a number of buttons in this chapter! But don't worry, we're almost through it.

Not long ago, I was listening to a speaker preach about possessions. He was very emphatic on the point of living simply. Just the bare necessities are all we need when we live in dependence upon God, he said. Whatever you bring in above that should be distributed among those who really need it.

There was a lot of truth in his message, speaking as he was to an affluent generation in one of the richest nations in the world's history. Jesus taught about loving and helping the poor. In fact, He said a great deal about generosity and sacrifice, asking the rich young ruler to sell his possessions and speaking of camels going through the eye of a needle. No one who is intellectually honest could've simply discarded the message this speaker delivered without at least giving it some sober thought.

Yet he became very specific – too specific. He offered dollar figures for the appropriate value of a Christian's house. He suggested what make and model of car we ought to drive, and where we should shop for inexpensive clothing. He had his details worked out and ready to prescribe. As I listened, I began to wonder if we were reading the same Bible! These were all disputable matters, items for every believer's personal judgment. It's very true that we can look at a culture blessed with abundant wealth and conclude that it should be more generous. Our funding for local and world missions should be a cup running over, if we can spend what we do on entertainment and luxuries. Many of us could afford to do without a fourth television set or a third vacation, sure. These are general suggestions that can be submitted for our reflection and prayer.

But when someone tells you how many dollars you can spend on a home, well, in the words of the old saying, he has stopped preachin' and gone to meddlin'. We are to help, encourage, and challenge one another, but never to dictate to one another about disputable matters.

I know some Christians who choose to live very simply, and God blesses them in so many ways. I also know some believers who are not guilt-stricken for the affluence that has come to them. Some of them live in fine homes and drive beautiful and often expensive cars. They also tend to make very generous contributions to ministries and charitable organizations. They understand that to whom much is given, much is required, and they respond by blessing others frequently and liberally. And they've learned that when we give, we ourselves are blessed more than the recipients of those gifts.

Financial wealth can be a means by which God empowers us to bless each other. It was a wealthy man who courageously came forward to offer his own tomb for the burial of Jesus. Do you think this was by chance, or was God using the resources he had already entrusted to Joseph of Arimathea? It's not money that is evil, according to Paul in his first letter to Timothy, but "the love of money" that is the root of all kinds of evil. So rather than insist that all believers divest of their wealth, we would do better to teach them that money can be a wonderful servant; it's just a horrible master.

The Meaning of a Gift

A young couple in our church cherished a piece of real estate they owned. They held it in trust for the future, for a time when they could build a dream home on that land. They were coming to church, identifying with our vision, and hearing about a wonderful facility we wanted to build in order to reach more people with the gospel. The couple felt

God's Spirit whispering for them to respond with unusual generosity, and they sold their land and donated all of the proceeds to help us build our facility.

It was a moving, emotional experience on so many levels, because it was truly sacrificial. We know from the story of Jesus about the widow's mite that it's not the specific amount given that matters, but the heartfelt desire to support the kingdom of God sacrificially. There are some people who are so rich they could have built our facility with their own funds and never felt a thing. That wouldn't have been sacrificial for them, just a huge write off. This young couple donated a dream, and none of us has anything more precious to give than our dream. "We don't need to build our house right now," they said. "It's the house of God that's most important."

Their gift, which totaled nearly one million dollars, was the largest single amount given during our capital campaign. They gifted us with their dream to help us fulfill ours: a worship center that for years now has served as a soul saving, life changing station in the Bay Area of northern California, a region that desperately needs dynamic Christian communities. Thousands of people have come to Christ in the facility. You could say that what they did was not crazy at all but very wise, because they converted the possible comfort of two people to the eternal blessing of many.

Meanwhile, even as we celebrate that victory of godly giving, a widow places her pennies in the plate. And God smiles just as broadly. In his power, he will bless that gift just as he blesses one worth hundreds of thousands of dollars. You see, we can't place a dollar value on these things. What is rich and what is poor? It depends upon how you look at it, and what you've experienced. For us it's a disputable matter, but for God it's not a matter at all. He owns everything. He sees value not so much in dollars and coins, but in *hearts*. That's what we must learn. All these things we argue about, all these disputable issues that seem so all-consuming and complicated and controversial—for God, it's much simpler. He looks at the human heart and at what we can become if we simply drop our weapons, join our hands, and begin worshiping and praising him together—whatever kind of music we use, whatever kind of car we drove to church in. It's all the same to him, because he is our Father and we are his children. He wants us to start building bridges and find the joy of connection.

In the end, that's the only thing we can really assume— that in all things, God wants what is best for us and is working for our good. Knowing that this is true, how can we find it within us to continue quarreling among ourselves?

6.

Accountability: Speaking and Hearing the Truth in Love

Several years ago, economist Steven Levitt wrote a best-selling book called *Freakonomics*. He applied a little bit of creativity to an exploration of how people and money function in unlikely places, from a sumo wrestling tournament to a downtown drug deal—as well as in Paul Feldman's bagel business.

Feldman is one of these fellows who goes from office to office, distributing his snack foods to break rooms and business kitchens. What's interesting is that he works completely on the honor system. He leaves his bagels and trusts people to leave their money. I suppose it all works out well enough for him to make a living. But there is an interesting insight in what Paul Feldman has discovered: Smaller offices are more honest, as groups, than bigger ones. Feldman can show you his ledger book to prove the point. The smaller groups can be counted on to pay for their bagels or even to overpay. If any dishonesty goes on, it tends to come from the larger settings.

That may not seem like such a big deal, until you think about it. In the large office. coffee breaks tend to take place in one particular section, and twenty or thirty people can gather in the break area at any given time, enjoying snacks and an informal conversation. There are a lot more witnesses to see whether someone dropped his money in the bagel box. In the small office, there would be more opportunities for folks to be in the break room by themselves, giving them chances to grab that snack without paying or being seen.

Feldman says it works out in just the opposite way. The business with a few dozen employees generally follows the honor system more than the one with a few hundred workers. In *Freakonomics*, Steven Levitt explains it by making a comparison to street crime. In the smaller town, there is less crime for various reasons—one of them being that people know each other and hold each other accountable. In the big city, we all know that crimes can happen with people walking right by, not wanting to get involved.

The point is that we live in a completely different way when we are in a setting of high accountability, where we are well known. When we get into smaller groups and experience real community, we generally make each other better people. We can encourage one another, challenge one another, protect one another, and hold one another accountable.

Ultimately, that's the kind of community Paul is talking about in his letter to the Romans. Throughout this book we've seen that he's telling his readers to stop thinking about technical points of belief, and start thinking about real people. Now keep in mind that this comes in the book of Romans, which is the most detailed explanation of Christian theology in the entire New Testament. Romans goes to the very heart of all that we believe as Christians. It lays out the details. It dots every i and crosses every t. Paul is definitely not afraid to lay out the very specific details of our most crucial beliefs.

But Paul makes a very important distinction between, say, the importance of the resurrection of Christ—an indisputable, line-in-the-sand essential—and what holidays should be celebrated by Christians, or what foods are kosher. And on these latter issues, Paul's guiding truth is this: When the principles aren't worthy of argument, we put people first. Once we have the key ingredients of the faith agreed upon, nothing is more important than our unity. Nothing is more important than community except the core truths that makes that community possible.

So Paul is telling us to look toward our influence upon one another. As long as we agree on the large stuff, we should not sweat the small stuff—not to the point of constant squabbles among ourselves. Protect that closeness, that love, that helps us to be people of integrity—people who pay for their bagels even when no one's looking, because the community has shaped us as people of integrity.

Sylvester Stallone, the Hollywood actor who has become Rocky and Rambo, has made this point recently, believe it or not. He had lived life in the fast lane since the mid-70s, when the classic underdog boxing film *Rocky* made him an international star. He lived his share of the red carpet life, made his share of poor decisions. But Stallone now says that in his confusion and disappointment with himself, he has wandered back to church and found blessing. Here is what "Rocky" says he has found in the body of Christ: "Church is the gym of the soul." In other words, good people give him a good workout on the inside, just like pounding on those sides of beef in the movie aided his physical training. His testimony is that fellow believers whip his soul into shape, make him better, stronger, able to take the enemy's blows.

Let's find out what Paul says about the "gym of the soul."

Mutual Edification

As Romans 14 continues, Paul brings this issue of relationship maintenance to a head. He finally classifies these petty squabbles as what they are: "stumbling blocks."

What exactly is a stumbling block? We see this phrase crop up in various parts of the Bible, from the book of Leviticus up through Paul's letters. Have you ever turned off the lights in your home, then had to grope to the bedroom in the darkness? You'd think we'd plan that moment a little better, but it happens! And Junior has left his building blocks on the floor so that you stumble over one of them. That's a stumbling "block."

In the ancient times, of course, people tripped over stones at night. When the devil tempted Jesus in the wilderness, he quoted a psalm that says the angels will lift the psalmist up in their hands, "so that you will not strike your foot against a stone" (Psalm 91:12). No one likes to stub a toe. That's why, in Leviticus 19:14, there was a command never to put a stumbling block in the path of a blind man; never to curse at a deaf man. A stumbling block, you see, is something that exploits someone's limitations. If you can't see, it's unfair for someone to block your path. If you can't hear, it's wrong for someone to say nasty things about you. And if your Bible-based belief system is routed in a certain direction, it's wrong for someone else to cross it up.

Now there's an interesting point here. Paul uses the idea of the stumbling block on more than one occasion. He uses it here, talking about it as something to avoid because it causes people to trip. But in other letters, he talks about the crucifixion of Jesus Christ being a stumbling block to Jews. Their belief system, you see, was routed in a certain direction so that God's promised deliverer should not walk, talk, or live like Jesus did. And he definitely should not die like a common criminal! By this logic, should we avoid talking about the crucifixion because it gives offense?

Far from it. We put no stumbling block in anyone's path, as Paul says—but God placed that one. I'm not just playing with words here. The cross is one of those essentials of our faith. That's a stumbling block the world must learn to confront, because God is the one who placed it there for a very good reason. Remember, this is a stone that you don't see in the dark. In fact, Jesus is referred to in Scripture as the Cornerstone, the stone the builder rejected.

Sometimes, however, we trip because we're walking in the darkness and in danger. In that case, a stumbling block is an important message. It's something to stop and consider. That's what the essentials of our faith are all about. Paul was a Hebrew scholar par excellence, and the new faith that worshiped Jesus was so much of a stumbling block that he helped hunt its people down and kill them. Paul "stumbled" right off his horse on the road to Damascus, and that was a good stumble. He tumbled right into the truth.

So there are good stumbling blocks as well as silly, unnecessary ones. Let's look at Paul's words on the silly ones:

Therefore let us stop passing judgment on one another. Instead, make up your mind not to put any stumbling block or obstacle in your brother's way. As one who is in the Lord Jesus, I am fully convinced that no food is unclean in itself. But if anyone regards something as unclean, then for him it is unclean. If your brother is distressed because of what you eat, you are no longer acting in love. Do not by your eating destroy your brother for whom Christ died. Do not allow what you consider good to be spoken of as evil. For the kingdom of God is not a matter of eating and drinking, but of righteousness, peace and joy in the Holy Spirit, because anyone who serves

Christ in this way is pleasing to God and approved by men.

Let us therefore make every effort to do what leads to peace and to mutual edification. Do not destroy the work of God for the sake of food. All food is clean, but it is wrong for a man to eat anything that causes someone else to stumble. It is better not to eat meat or drink wine or to do anything else that will cause your brother to fall.

So whatever you believe about these things keep between yourself and God. Blessed is the man who does not condemn himself by what he approves. But the man who has doubts is condemned if he eats, because his eating is not from faith; and everything that does not come from faith is sin.

(Romans 14:13-23)

Handle With Care

These words leap out, don't they? "Don't destroy the work of God for the sake of food . . . The kingdom of God is not a matter of eating and drinking." Don't destroy the work of God for the sake of music style or plain issues of culture. Because, you see, we are the work of God. One of my favorite Bible verses says that we are God's handiwork, made to do good works in Him (Eph. 2:10).

There's an old legend about a small monastery that lay just outside a town. Over the years, it had grown smaller and smaller, as monks grew old and failed to recruit younger men to take their place. In time, the monks were losing their faith, because they saw nothing good happen. Finally they were down to three old men, who lived together in the old, dusty monastery where most of the houses were closed up. They spent most of their time bickering, and that was their insulated little world. Their names were Fathers Abbot, Babbot, and Cabbot.

One day a mysterious stranger, one who had the bearing of a wise and holy man, came to lodge for an evening in the monastery. He sat over dinner with the three old men and watched how impatient and tired of one another they seemed to be. He saw their complete lack of hope or vision, and sat silently until the three men asked him for a word of spiritual wisdom. The stranger said, "Here is my word for you. A great man is coming soon, the most powerful and significant prophet in hundreds of years. He will be revealed at any time, and he will be revealed in this place, because he is one of you."

The three old men were astonished! At first they thought it was a very bad joke, and they looked at one another incredulously. They sat stroking their gray beards, their hands trembling. For several days, they could hardly sleep. The outlandish idea began to take root. They were thinking: Which one of us is to be revealed as someone great? Father Abbot looked closely at Fathers Babbot and Cabbot, comparing the two. In some ways, he could see slightly more good points in one than the other; then, when he considered again, it seemed just the opposite. Father Babbot scrutinized Abbot and Cabbot, picking up on little virtues he had never noticed. Father Cabbot was watching the other two, wondering how he had missed the little hints of shrewd wisdom and benevolence.

All three men were paying close attention to each other, watching for the time when one of them would be revealed—and, in being watched, each of them found himself on his best behavior. There were no more of the customary squabbles. As a matter of fact, compliments flew back and forth the way insults had once done, because each of the three were watching closely for hidden virtues, watching for the signs of a wonderful prophet.

A kind of attractive holiness began to shine from the relationships of these men, and it was noticed by people from the town as they came and went, passing by on the road. And young people began to come and sit at the feet of the men, just to listen to the wisdom and see the honor they bestowed upon one another. Some of them were initiated as new monks. And for the first time in many generations, the monastery pulsed with life and energy again—all because these three old men were looking for the goodness in each other. In the years that came, people tended to forget the prediction of a great prophet, but they remembered that during that time, there were three very holy men at the old monastery.

You see, we are God's handiwork—not potentially, not possibly; we are God's handiwork *right now.* All true believers are children of the kingdom, heirs to God's kingdom. All of us are hosts to the Holy Spirit, who has come to live not only within us but among us as we spend time together.

Christianity today is too often like the shrinking, dying huddle of bickering saints who have lost their vision—and we wonder why outsiders don't want to come and be part of us. We sit around in our churches rearranging the stumbling blocks and watching each other trip over them. What we need is to begin seeing Christ in each other's eyes. "Where two or three come together in my name," Jesus said, "there am I with them." And it's a beautiful thing to see how he can cause us to see the best in each other, and push us toward that potential—when we do it right. When we do it wrong, things get ugly.

So this is what we're saying: It's not only about avoiding certain subjects that start arguments; it's also about what we can do positively and proactively to make each other, and make our relationships, even stronger. It's about intentionally building bridges.

We can start with the right kind of accountability.

Real Accountability

There's a right way and a wrong way to help guide other people. When we get it right, we can make an incredible difference in the life of someone else.

Maybe you remember that movie *The Green Mile* that came out years ago. The director was Frank Darabont, and the movie was a big hit. Afterward, Darabont gave an interview in which he was asked what he would remember about the shooting of *The Green Mile*. He said that fifteen or twenty years in the future, he would still remember how Tom Hanks worked with lesser known actors. The film introduced Michael Clarke Duncan, a huge man who played the unjustly accused prisoner.

As the camera was rolling for a key scene, said Darabont, it was focused on Duncan first. But the director was surprised to see something going on just off-camera. Tom Hanks, he said, was delivering an Academy Award-worthy performance for Duncan—even though Hanks was not on camera—to provide every possible dramatic nuance that Duncan could play off to get the right acting in the scene. In other words, Hanks knew this wasn't his screen time—but he injected his very best acting skill to help the younger man give a better performance.

"He wanted Michael to do so well," said Darabont. "He wanted him to look so good. I'll never forget that." A few months later, Michael Clarke Duncan was nominated for an Academy Award for Best Actor in a Supporting Role. Tom Hanks, however, didn't receive a nomination. He'd won a couple of Oscars by this time, and for him it was all about helping someone else be the best he could be.

That's accountability done right. We're not so caught up in ourselves; we don't care whether the camera is always on us, but we're doing all that we can for the other person.

We all like the idea of helping each other become all that they can be—at least in theory. At the office, someone reports to you and you hold them responsible for making a certain number of sales calls, or getting a certain number of reports done. The problem, for many of us, comes when we discover that we have to look up the chain as well as down—someone is just above, holding us accountable, too.

This is the give-and-take of life. The whole social fabric breaks down when we mess this up. For example, when people stop being accountable to the laws, you have crime. Likewise, when Christians stop following biblical patterns for doing church in a loving way, you have a dysfunctional body of believers. The Old Testament has a little shorthand statement that always signals that a mess is about to happen in Israel: "Everyone did what was right in his own eyes." Some people think that's the American Way, independence and self-reliance and all—but the truth is, our own eyes see with less than 20/20 vision when it comes to righteousness. God has built in social checks and balances, and we call this the system of accountability. We are to use both eyes to look out for one another.

When our systems get fouled up, it's usually because we've gone to one of two extremes. One is the extreme of harshness. "I'm going to hold you accountable by controlling your life" is how this one goes. "You just stop thinking and do exactly what I tell you. I'll handle everything."

Now think about this: What happens when we set up a little society of harsh accountability—in other words, one person or a small group controlling every thought and movement of everyone else? We call that a cult. People go off to some kind of little commune and do everything the great leader tells them to, and of course he never tells them to do rational things, or things that benefit anyone but himself, the leader. Eventually it could cost people their lives, as it has done in a couple of tragic situations—with Jim Jones at

Jonestown, or the tragedy in Waco. At the very least, harsh accountability costs people their personhood; it takes away that special individuality God gave them. We are his children, his custom handiwork, as unique and individual as our fingerprints. We are not made to walk in lockstep, thinking and saying what we are told.

But it doesn't have to happen in a classic cult setting, off in some strange camp. It happens in churches, too. Misguided Christian leaders build their own little kingdoms, make their own little disciples, by exerting an unhealthy amount of intimidation and control over someone who is willing to accept that, for some reason or other.

You shouldn't be out of control of your own life—that is, if you are an adult, no other human being should have full say-so over what you do. Only God, through his Holy Spirit, should have that level of authority for you. Of course you have a boss at work, perhaps two parents, teachers at school, a spiritual leader—whatever situation you're in, you're under some kind of authority. But you shouldn't abandon complete control to another person if you're a grownup. When someone comes along to help us grow, they do so with love and respect. They encourage; they reason; they allow us to make a few mistakes and learn things for ourselves. As a matter of fact, good parents do this; good pastors; good bosses at work. We, the leaders, always get better results when we work through love rather than force.

In a previous chapter I gave the example of a speaker giving out detailed instructions for how much people should spend for this or that. I don't believe this is God's intention for spiritual authority. A leader's job is to point you toward the truth in spiritual principles from the Word, and let the Holy Spirit guide you in the specifics. Control is not account- ability. We must give freedom.

But control is only one of the two extremes that is the mistake. Let's discover the opposite mistake.

Tough Enough?

We don't want to intimidate or overpower someone to hold them accountable. But what happens if we go too far in the other direction? The opposite of harsh accountability would be hands-off accountability.

After all, as much as we want to be gentle and accommodating, there do come times for tough love. Proverbs 27:5-6 reads, "Better is open rebuke than hidden love. Wounds from a friend can be trusted, but an enemy multiplies kisses."

Open rebuke, of course, is another phrase for tough love: it sounds mean, but it has the best intentions and may be the only thing to say in a difficult spot. Hidden love is really weak love. In fact, I would argue that it's not much love at all, because when we need it most, it backs down. Leaders miss their goal when they surround themselves with yes-men and yes-women, people who say only what they want to hear. The wisest CEOs, pastors, presidents and leaders have a couple of people around them who may be irritating at times, but they can help the leader see things from a different perspective. They say what must be said. Or put another way: they speak the truth in love. That's what Paul exhorts us to do in Ephesians 4:15.

I like the proverb, "wounds from a friend can be trusted." Have you ever felt wounded by a friend? Here's the difference: An enemy will stab you in the back; a friend will cut you in the front, before your eyes. An enemy stabs to inflict pain with a knife of hatred or malice, but a friend cuts surgically with a scalpel of unfeigned love, to remove something that needs to come out. Everybody needs a little doctoring every now and then, a little minor surgery. On the other hand, when someone's going to cut into us, we need a little anesthesia, don't we? Thankfully, a doctor won't walk right up to you and stab right in! He's going to prepare you; he's going to make an appointment and say, "come at this time, and here's what you should do to prepare." He's going to speak gently to you and also let your loved ones know how the surgery is going. And he's going to help you recover afterwards.

When we give "wounds to a friend," we need to do everything a good doctor would do. We do well to prepare the person, not just dive in like a kamikaze attack. "There's something I'd like to speak with you about. When would be a good time for us to sit down and put our heads together?" we might ask. And generally speaking, we shouldn't "operate" without permission—that means earning a level of trustworthy friendship with that individual. We need to apply the anesthesia of gentle words and careful handling. We need to cooperate with other people who know our friend, just as the doctor talks to the family. Finally we need to help our friend get going again. You see? Tough love can actually be tender.

But there do have to be boundaries. We do have to step up and love someone enough to tell them what they don't want to hear, even to risk their getting a little angry with us. It's just human nature that people recoil from criticism in the beginning. They hear what we're saying more than they may indicate, so we shouldn't be completely put off by their initial sensitivity to "the wounds of a friend." We have to be strong and say what must be said.

It's particularly true for parents—and this is precisely where I often get myself into trouble with permissive moms and dads who seem clueless about why God gave them children! Some people resist this message, but it's true: *We are ruining a generation in the name of love.*

Parents are abdicating their responsibility to hold their children accountable; I see it far too often. Yes, we know the Bible says parents should not exasperate their children, and we don't want to drive them away from home in bitterness when they get old enough to leave. But we also don't want to let them run wild, because that will destroy them even more quickly. Many parents today have a difficult time setting the limits and holding the line. We can be strict and still loving. We can uphold good, wise discipline and still be tender and positive and supportive with our children.

But when we allow them to make the laws around the house, when we become intimidated by their tantrums or threats, then we are failing to prepare them to live happy and responsible lives as adults. My counsel to our parents is to be loving, set clear limits, and hold your children account-able to stay on the right side of those limits. That's ultimately what they want us to do anyway.

Your Inner Circle

Now that we've talked about right accountability vs. harsh accountability and hands-off accountability, I'd like you to please think about the people around you: friends, family, fellow believers. Who keeps you going the right way, with the most helpful mix of toughness and tenderness? Who should hold you accountable, but does not? Is there anybody who tries to control you?

To be sure, not everyone in your life needs to be a no-nonsense force of discipline in our lives. Some simply aren't close enough, or comfortable enough, to be part of your accountability circle. That's fine. We can and should have some casual acquaintances in life who don't really go shoulder-to-shoulder with us in the foxholes in life's field of battle.

But we don't need any of those who go to the other extreme, trying to control every move. It only takes one of those to make life miserable! There are people who suffer through their friendships instead of enjoying them. For some reason, they run with control-freak companions for years, doing everything that other person wants them to do. There's no reason we should live that kind of life. Christ has set us free from condemnation, and our freedom in Christ should never be usurped by fellow believers who seek to manipulate us with their words, actions, and attitudes. So how can you deal with the control-freaks? My advice is to simply talk to them. Say, "I love you, I appreciate you, but I can't allow you to continue speaking into my life because it's just too difficult. My life has enough misery without my friendships adding more. You try to control me, and only God can have that level of authority over my life. If you think this is something that can change, then let's talk. Otherwise, I have to step back, and I hope you'll understand." Speak your mind and heart, speak it in love, and if your friend doesn't change, then pray for him or her.

How about in marriage? You can't tell your spouse you can no longer hang out together—not if you want to do things God's way. Again, speak the truth in love. Say, "If we're going to make this marriage work, we need to love one another without trying to exert control or domination. I'm struggling with how much you want to call every shot, tell me what I can think or do." Having said this, commit it to God and see if you get good results. If your marriage continues to struggle, get good counsel from your pastor or a counselor with a biblical worldview. It's so important to learn the right medium between freedom and accountability in any relationship.

Can you be controlled by your children? Many parents are, as I've already indicated. Maybe the time has come to sit down and say, "Son, daughter, I've done wrong by you. I haven't been preparing you for the harshness of this world. If you always get your way around here, you'll think it's going to be the same way out there. It will be a crushing experience, you can trust me on that. We, your parents, need to love you enough to hold you accountable. I want you to know that we're going to do a better job establishing boundaries and calling you to respect them, not because we're trying to make your life miserable, but because we're trying to bring you joy in the long run." Oh, you may get some rolled eyes and sarcastic remarks—for the moment. But they appreciate it more than they'll show. In their heart-of-hearts, deep in their souls, they want their parents to guide them. They crave that accountability. And one day they will bless your name for it. And even if they don't, you'll have the satisfaction of knowing that you acted in their best interests.

Finally, prayerfully open your heart so that God can bless you to develop one or more true friendships—persons who will love you at the highest level of trust. Share your heart with such persons and charge them with the responsibility of calling you on it when you get out of line. It takes real strength to offer real vulnerability. But we have to do it, because we all have our blind spots.

Have you ever thought about blind spots in driving? The best driver has that little zone behind him where he can't see if another car is there. When the driver tries to shift into another lane, someone else in the car might have to quickly shout, "No!" At that split second, the driver will stay in his lane, and he may be a little peeved at the person who shouted in his ear right in the middle of conversation—until he realizes that the watchful passenger, who could see into the driver's blind spot, may have helped to avoid an accident. Then, if the driver has any sense, he'll say, "Thanks for yelling at me just when you did."

Too many of us drive alone in life. No one is there to keep an eye on the blind spot. No one is there to shout, "No!"—a bit abruptly, but necessarily—when we swerve toward calamity. Who watches out for you? Is there a friend who "sticks closer than a brother," as the biblical proverb puts it? If you're a single adult, and you're thinking about making a questionable, if not outright stupid, marry decision, who in your life is courageous enough to step up and tell you that it's going to be a big mistake? Are you going to say, "It's none of your business," and reward that friend by cutting him or her off—or will you listen?

In our church family, my pastoral staff and I highly endorse pre-engagement counseling. But an everyday friend can sometimes see better and more closely than even we do as counselors. He or she has seen you when you didn't know they were watching. They've observed your prospective mate as well. Counselors are great, but we need can never have too much of the right kind of accountability.

Core Values

Perhaps the greatest fielding shortstop in baseball history was Ozzie Smith of the St. Louis Cardinals. On July 28, 2002, he was inducted into the Baseball Hall of Fame. He made an acceptance speech that we all need to hear, and it has nothing to do with whether or not you like baseball.

Smith compared the structure of his life to the construction of a baseball. The ball has a cork center. That center is the true ball—it's who he, Ozzie Smith, really is or would like to be. Protecting the center are two distinct rubber shells. For Smith, these are his faith in God and the faith in himself that came through the encouragement of a loving mother in his life.

Next in the cross-section of that baseball, we find two hundred yards of wool wrapped around the rubber shells and the core. Smith sees these as "strands of love and faith that so many other people have wrapped around Ozzie Smith as a person, and wrapped around my dream through their love and faith in me."

Smith said, "I will never forget the faith that my high school coach, Art Webb . . . had in me. Just about the time I was questioning my ability and expressed thoughts of going home, Art got wind of my feelings, called me up, and sternly told me, 'Oz, you're not going to quit. You're going to hang in there and weather the storm!' And because of that...I stayed." Art Webb did accountability right.

We all want to be "wrapped in love" the way Ozzie Smith feels he has been—faith in God at the center, then surrounded by strands of support that have just the right tension. Nothing is softer than wool; it's like being wrapped in a warm sweater. But if that wool is too loosely wrapped, the baseball won't go five feet when you hit it. Spalding will reject it for the Major Leagues. And if the wool is too tight, too pressured, the very core will be crushed.

Oswald Chambers said something about that: "When you meet a man or woman who puts Jesus Christ first, knit that one to your soul."

I'd say that "wraps up" this chapter, wouldn't you?

7.

Accommodation: Protecting the Weaker Ones

Our church is located in northern California, in what is called the San Francisco Bay Area. I moved here in 1989, an unforgettable year for those who lived in this area at the time. And no, it wasn't because of my arrival! Believe me, my early days of ministry on the west coast didn't cause the slightest movement on the Richter Scale. But an earthquake that shook the '89 World Series certainly did.

For the first and only time, baseball had a Bay Bridge series between the San Francisco Giants and Oakland Athletics. You can imagine the excitement around here—and then the earthquake came. It arrived with Game 3 and suspended the Series for ten days. There was a shift in one of the fault lines, and the resulting quake killed several dozen people, injured thousands, and left many more homeless.

The Apostle Paul tells us, "We know that the whole creation has been groaning as in the pains of childbirth right up to the present time" (Romans 8:22). Not only are humans fallen and flawed on this side of heaven, but the physical world itself awaits its redemption upon the return of Christ. I'm convinced that the earthquake was not God reaching down to punish the Bay Area for sin. After all, if God were going after sinners, we wouldn't have stopped with northern California! Instead, the quake was a physical spasm on a fallen planet that is filled with fallen people. It was also an important reminder to all people of the coming judgment when each person will give an account to God. So when disasters drive people to the Bible, to prayer, and to the church, I tend to say "Amen" and get ready to minister to those who show up in search of God.

Back to 1989. The Lord was in the early stages of transforming my ministry and the church he called me to lead. It had exactly 34 members when I arrived in California that year. I had left my pastorate at a large and vibrant congregation in my hometown of Philadelphia to come here, to work with a small African-American congregation that wanted to grow. That year, I saw a film that yielded a phrase I came to embrace: *If you build it, he will come.* Yes, you've got it: baseball again. That was a line from a movie *Field of Dreams* with Kevin Costner. The main character had a vision to build a baseball diamond in a cornfield, and he was obedient to that vision. He built it and "he" came: Shoeless Joe Jackson, an old ballplayer from many decades ago, returned from oblivion to play baseball again.

The "he" in my vision was not Shoeless Joe, but Christ. We knew if we built it—a church that loved God and others deeply—he would come and fulfill the vision he gave me of seeing thousands of people become born again and mature into fully devoted followers of Christ. But just as Costner's character was called to go against the grain (pardon the pun) of an Iowa cornfield and put a baseball diamond in it, we found the Holy Spirit going against the grain of church demographic trends. Most churches in America are homogenous, i.e., characterized by one predominant racial group, and we tend to be quite accepting of that norm. You know—birds of a feather flock together, that kind of thing.

I was too. In moving to California, I fully expected that the thousands the Lord would bless our church to reach would be African American like the 34 members who called me to be their pastor! But the Lord began to build a church that today is thoroughly multi-racial, and full of generational, socio-economic, and educational diversity as well. We are a veritable "United Nations" under Christ, a church where rich and poor, notable leaders and everyday Joes, PhDs and "GEDs" are held in equal regard and enjoy fellowship with each other. And along the way, we have learned the importance of consciously agreeing on the essentials while consciously avoiding stumbling blocks. And the result has been both spiritual and relational growth that we could've never imagined.

Thinking back to the 1989 earthquake, I realize that it can be totally explained in geological terms—a natural disaster. But what has happened in our church is nothing short of *supernatural*. I certainly could never do it through my own limited skills. It's a God thing. Period. And he has used it to teach me that unity does not require uniformity. It requires building bridges that help us accommodate one another.

Five-Star Accommodations

Throughout this section of Paul's letter, we've seen this theme of bearing with one another, accepting one another, accommodating one another. Or conversely, in negative terms, do *not* be arrogant; do not assume; do not attempt to control other people. In the first verse of Romans 14, Paul has told us to accommodate the faith of those who are weak—the "newbies" of God's kingdom.

Mark De Ymaz is another pastor of a multi-ethnic, economically diverse church. His congregation, Mosaic Church of Central Arkansas. He has written a book called *Building a Healthy Multi-Ethnic Church*, in which he compares a multi-ethnic church to a simple family that spans several generations. Let's say that Grandma is still alive and in pretty good health, and she has moved in with you, your spouse, and several children. The family dinner table is an important tradition of your family. When dinner is served, everyone comes to the table. That's the best time for family communication.

Now, tonight, Grandma has come into the kitchen a little early. She's helping feed the baby while you and your spouse set the table. That's when Junior and his sister walk into the room, arguing over who gets to watch their favorite TV program. They sit down and suspend their argument for the time when someone says the blessing. But the older son, a teenager, is missing. You climb the stairs and find him playing a video game with headphones on. You get his attention and say, "Didn't you hear us call you for dinner?"

"Sure," he replies. "But I'm not coming. It's meat loaf, and I don't like it."

The pastor says that when he gives this example, he always stops and asks, "As a parent, how would you respond?" He says that he has never gotten any answer other than the following: Tell the son to come to the table whether he's eating or not. Lesson: It's not about the food but the family.

You would probably say something like, "Son, family dinner is the one command performance around our house. It's not about eating; we have breakfast and lunch at different times and places. But this is the one meal we can have together, the best time for us to look into each other's eyes, talk about what's important, and maintain our precious and unique *family-ness*. We're making memories, and they're not complete if you're not with us. And by the way, you'll approve of tomorrow night's menu: pizza."

Grandma enjoys the meat loaf, but tomorrow night, she will be the one who struggles with the main course. Her stomach won't easily digest pizza. However, no one has to insist that she come to the table on that evening, because she is more mature, more far-sighted. She understands what that dinner table is all about, and derives joy from watching the young ones savor their pepperoni slices. Her priorities transcend food.

That's what accommodation is all about. We learn to see the forest, not just the trees. We perceive the big picture of what God is doing, and that lends us tolerance. I think about my own grandmother accommodating the younger ones who wanted drums in the church. Her ears weren't tickled by the sound of drums, but she enjoyed the passion of the kids playing their own sounds that lifted up Christ. She knew she was a part of something bigger than her taste in music—something that would move deeper into the future than her own life.

Here's another beautiful, godly word: *deference.* When we defer to one another, that's a way of bowing to a fellow believer at the doorway, giving a little wave of the hand, and saying, "After you, my friend." You know that look that you see on an elderly woman's face when a young person holds a door open for her? That quick, unexpected smile of pleasure, the delighted twinkle in the eyes?

That's what accommodation and deference do in the body of Christ. They say, "We are different, but we are the same. One of us is old, one is young, but before God we are eternal and ageless. One of us is black, one is white, but God loves us all." That's exciting, and it should make us willing to be patient and accommodating.

Word of the Weak

We've said a lot in this book about differences of belief on disputable matters. But Paul is also talking about the weak and the strong. Here's the point: A genuine, God-breathed fellowship will always be attracting new believers, and they won't emerge into God's kingdom as fully-formed, doctrinally advanced church members. They will be finding their way, and at the very least, they will need our patience. At the very most, they will need our sacrificial attention as their friends, guides, and mentors. Some of them have not learned what the Scriptures teach, and for many, your life will be the first Bible they read. You are the present physical picture of what this faith is all about, so you want to be at your very best, to represent God's grace to someone who has seen little of it.

Again, using the example of family, think about what a parent does. When little ones enter the home, we "childproof" every room. That means going around and removing the stumbling blocks. We put dangerous things high on shelves or mantles. We don't let our children have toys or small objects that they might swallow. When they are around, we don't watch certain movies or shows that they may not be emotionally prepared to see. It's just a matter of being a loving parent. We want our children to have the best possible environment for growing into healthy adults. When they're two years old and become mobile, at first we follow them all over the room. Have you ever done that? Remember what it's like? The little one learns to look curiously to you before reaching for something, to see if you'll smile or if you'll say, "No!"

There might be times, after your child has gone to bed, that you watch a TV show that could have a somewhat violent scene or something that would upset the child. I've heard a few parents say, "Oh, I just let it all hang out with my children. I expose them to everything and let them get used to it." I say that's extremely unwise, and likely dangerous! Why? Because it exposes children to confusion and causes great anxiety and disruption in their lives. An adult, who has worked out what he or she can or can't handle, is capable of managing certain things. But wisdom and love would dictate that you wouldn't flaunt those things in front of the young.

As the child grows into teenage years, he has more freedom. You don't go every single place the child goes, but you're keeping tabs. You try to be certain your teen has a healthy set of friends, does the right things, and stays in wholesome environments. Eventually, he will be an adult and responsible for all his own actions. He will leave the home, whether tearfully or bounding out of the house with tremendous excitement, and your greatest prayer will be that he has the wisdom and maturity to live a godly and fruitful life.

It's really not much different in the church, God's family. The "weaker" brothers and sisters need us to watch over them a bit more closely. We must guide them gently toward the healthier influences. And throughout the years of their spiritual development, we'll have had to accommodate them. Here is how Paul phrases it:

We who are strong ought to bear with the failings of the weak and not to please ourselves. Each of us should please his neighbor for his good, to build him up. For even Christ did not please himself but, as it is written: "The insults of those who insult you have fallen on me." For everything that was written in the past was written to teach us, so that through endurance and the encouragement of the Scriptures we might have hope.

(Romans 15:1-4)

Again, Paul says, you have freedom. You know what you can or can't handle as a Christian. But don't flaunt it in front of the weak who are still learning to walk in faith. Don't worry only about yourself and what pleases you, but about your fellow believers and what is needful for them. With great position comes great responsibility.

Let's say you have a big, sturdy coffee mug. It gets everyday use and is cleaned in the dishwasher regularly. The little picture on the outside is beginning to fade, and it gets knocked around at times. But that's all right. You still count on it and use it almost absent-mindedly while talking on the phone, reading, or working. But you wouldn't think of using fine china the same way. If you had special guests to dinner and decide to break out the china, you'd expect everyone at the table to be careful how they picked it their elegant tea cups, put them down; and you certainly wouldn't want to see one knocked to the floor! Why? Because they're delicate; yes, weak, and that's actually what makes it precious and special.

Our "delicate" brothers and sisters are precious and special too. We might treat ourselves, the experienced saints, a little more casually. But we have to be on guard with the weaker ones, and we must accommodate them.

Getting It Backwards

Now, as with most biblical principles, we have a tendency to turn this idea upside down and stand it on its head. I'll give an example from my youthful days.

You could hunt down certain photographs of me that were taken during the early 70s. I know those pictures are out there somewhere, and they prove that I had an impressive Afro haircut "back in the day." If you weren't around in those days, you'd have to watch a few old television shows (maybe "The Mod Squad") to know what I'm talking about. But if you're a certain age, you've got the picture.

I was a teenager, I was a part of a certain time and certain fashions, and I was into my hair. I would braid it at night, pick it out in the morning, and leave home sporting an Afro that I figured would impress the girls! I was saved and completely unaware of generational differences regarding how men should wear their hair. So I proudly brought myself to church, basketball Afro and all. But one day an elderly lady, one of the saints of our church, walked up to me and said, "You know what, young man? Your hair offends me." She wasn't a fan of Motown music, and she certainly couldn't understand why a Christian young man would want to copy the hairstyles of the Jackson Five and some of the other black artists of that era.

As a young believer, I was taken aback by those words. I went to my father and reported what had been said. I asked if I needed to get a haircut just to make your happy. "No, son, you don't," he told me—which was wonderful news to my ears, because I was immature and vulnerable, and being forced to conform to someone's demands other than Christ's may well have driven me away from the very fellowship that I needed to help me grow.

My dad had a little meeting with some of the older saints, outside the presence of the younger ones. That was very wise. He didn't need to show them up in front of the young people, who would have cheered him on. He simply needed to be gentle and help those folks to see things from a different perspective.

I can imagine exactly what he had to say, because by now I've had to conduct a few of those meetings myself. People just forget that the church is a family, not a museum. It's about all of us *in process* toward becoming more like Christ (rather than each other's preconceptions) and this process is not always neat and orderly. I find that when people come to understand that, they cooperate for the most part. You help the older saints understand where the young ones are in their new walk; then you meet with the younger ones and say, "The older saints deserve your full respect. You may not always agree with their perspective, but I'd better not hear you mouthing off to them."

This type of conflict happens all the time in churches and families, but let's stop and think about it. The "strong" believer, in this case, was the elderly lady. She was saved long before I was even born. She rose each morning at 4:30 for prayer, and she read her Bible regularly. I was the "weaker" believer. Yet *I* was the stumbling block for *her*. I believe Paul would've said that we need to turn this one right-side up. Unless we define hairstyle as an essential Christian belief, then this would be an issue of accommodation for more mature believers. It should have been about whether her preferences were a stumbling block for me at that point—not the other way around. And today, I'm the one who must guard against presenting the obstacle. It just comes with the territory.

Today, we don't see Afros very much. But you could substitute any number of other fashions of the day: tattoos, piercings, hair dyed in colors not found in nature, low-slung, baggy pants; you can make your own list. The truth is that if we turn up the temperature prematurely on people because of the styles of their age and culture, we make it a little harder for them to learn what it means to follow Jesus. We can intimidate them right out the front door of the church and away from the one environment that can help them grow strong in faith. If we're going to risk doing that, we'd better have a serious conversation with ourselves first: Is this issue that offends us important enough to make it an obstacle to someone's spiritual development?

Taking the Blows

Therefore I don't like to hear about a wise, older believer playing the stumbling block card. That's simply a form of manipulation. We can always find something in the church that doesn't please us, then walk around and say, "Hey, you can't do that! It's a stumbling block for me."

The stumbling block issue can become another trump card, just another weapon of selfishness, while it's meant to be a safeguard for love. Paul is talking about bearing with one another, not being "bear"-like to one another. As a matter of fact, he tells us that instead of giving out the blows, we need to step up and absorb them on behalf of the weaker believers. In Romans 15:3, he writes, "For even Christ did not please himself but, as it is written: 'The insults of those who insult you have fallen on me.'"

He is quoting a psalm, and the idea is that we step forward like champions, to take on each other's pain and infirmity. Why? Because Christ did it for us. Remember, he serves as our model. He stands before the Father as our advocate, pleading our case. He did not say, "You know what? Your sins are a stumbling block for me. I don't like the way you act, the way you dress, the way you do anything at all. You're unacceptable until you clean your life up!" Rather, he took our sin fully upon himself, then sent us the Holy Spirit to teach us how to live for him.

At the Last Supper, Jesus got down on his hands and knees and washed dirty feet to provide a picture of loving leadership. He was saying, "You've walked all over this countryside in the heat of the day, picking up dust and filth. But have no fear; I'm going to clean you off."

During that supper, he started at the bottom, the dirtiest part, the feet. Then the following day, after being betrayed, humiliated, and beaten mercilessly, he stumbled to the cross...and washed the rest of us, right down to the soul.

Given what he's done for us, it's a no-brainer that we take care of each other with sacrificial love. Nobody is asking that you let yourself be nailed to a cross—only that you die to self and have patience with others who need time and accommodation to grow.

To obey this command from Romans, I must say, "The insults of those who insult you have fallen upon me." That means I've got your back. And your front. It means that when we see a brother or sister being hurt by life, we want to go out and absorb some of the pain ourselves. The more we learn to love, the more it feels instinctive, the way it is for moms and dads. Any loving parent would rather take the pain personally than see the child suffer.

This is how we bear up one another in the body of Christ. And the more we practice love rather than simply talk about it, the more attractive our faith will be to those who don't yet know the Savior. They must first experience love from us, and that love will be a gateway to the superior, limitless love of Christ. He won us by absorbing the blows for us on the cross. And those who would follow him must heed his words: "A new command I give you: Love one another. As I have loved you, so you must love one another. By this all men will know that you are my disciples, if you love one another" (John 13:34-35).

Carry That Weight

In Romans 15:1, when Paul writes, "We who are strong ought to bear with the failings of the weak," the word *bear* is crucial. In other verses of the New Testament, it means "to pick up and carry a weight." The other examples include bearing a pitcher of water, bearing the weight of a man, and bearing an obligation.

That's what being strong is all about, isn't it? What you're able to bear; what you can lift and carry forward. In Christianity, that's what we do in all things. We lift one another. We bear each other's burdens and worries. Sometimes we bear each other's bad moods and cross words. We forgive and love with increasing stubbornness. Otherwise we would be just like everybody else in the world. What would be so

special about the church without God's special love residing in our hearts and expressing itself through our words and actions?

Joni Eareckson Tada is a quadriplegic Christian, a beautiful person on the inside and the outside. She gives her life to encouraging disabled Christians and serving as their advocates in the church and other places.

Several years ago, just after the bombing of the federal building in Oklahoma City, she was invited to join a team of Christian counselors to minister to the survivors. She was eager to help. When she arrived on the scene, she reported to the American Red Cross center to check in. She wheeled her chair into the building and found people setting up chairs, arranging paper forms, and putting out doughnuts and coffee. Her eyes fell on a tall, dignified woman in a white lab coat, holding a clipboard.

When the woman saw Joni rolling into the room, a big smile came to her face. She said, "Oh, my, are we glad to see you here!"

Joni asked why.

The woman said, "When people walk up to you in your wheelchair and see you handle your personal crisis with that smile of yours, it speaks volumes to them. It assures them that they can handle their crisis, too. We need people like you in here. Please, help us go out and find more individuals like you who can assist us."

Joni later wrote that these words brought a beautiful picture to her mind. Wouldn't it be great it the church were like that? Wouldn't it be great if the hallways of our churches were crowded with new visitors hearing the same kind of greeting: "Are we glad to see you! We need people like you in this church who are ready to receive and then share with others the life changing love of Christ."

I think that would be a better greeting for a guest than, "I'm sorry, but you're sitting in my usual seat." I'd love to see us bear with one another rather than be bear-like with one another. Wouldn't you?

After all, someone is bearing with you. You're no more perfect than me or anyone else. You might not be limited by a wheelchair, but I'm sure there's something else about you that requires the patience of others.

Listen to some other words by Paul about our weakness:

> *The eye cannot say to the hand, "I don't need you!"*
> *And the head cannot say to the feet, "I don't need*
> *you!" On the contrary, those parts of the body that*
> *seem to be weaker are indispensable, and the parts*
> *that we think are less honorable we treat with special*
> *honor.*
>
> *(1 Corinthians 12:21-23)*

In the end, you see, we are not free agents. We are all parts of one body, all indispensible. Maybe the eyes are a little near-sighted, but we keep them anyway. Maybe the hand has lost a finger in some accident; we still have nine good fingers, and we value them all the more once we've lost one.

That's the way it is with the church. There is one head and a host of supporting parts, every one of them weak in some way. The head is Christ, and only he receives glory. The rest of us support each other, or we are something less than the body of Christ. Somehow, through a miracle of God, together we are strong and divinely enabled to do His will. United we stand, divided we're a mess!

I challenge you to take inventory of your relationships. There are people you love and cherish, but what about those who are difficult to bear? What about those you would rather not be around, but have to? It could be someone at work; it could be someone at church or a next-door neighbor. I would be very surprised if you can't list five people in your life whom you find it a challenge to love.

Go ahead and make the list. Write them down—I'm not talking about general principles anymore, I'm talking about your life! When I'm preaching, I like to say, "I'm not talking about you, but someone on your row." But you're the reader right now, and you don't have to be embarrassed because I'm not there with you physically. It's just you, God, and this book. So there's no reason you can't get out paper and pencil and make that list.

Have you done it? Good. Now look at each name. Which have flaws or weaknesses or little irritating habits that have to be accommodated? Now—which people on your list are objects of God's love?

Let me guess—all of the people have flaws, weaknesses, or irritating habits...and all of them are loved by God. Am I right?

Then here is part B of this exercise. Pray over each name—carefully and reflectively. Ask God to help you love every single one the way he does. As you yield your body and soul to him, he will answer that prayer. I've never known him to hold out when someone seeks to be a conduit of his love toward others. Ask God to help you love them through his Holy Spirit rather than your limitations. And finally, look for an opportunity to serve each person; even to take a blow or two on their behalf if necessary. Take one for the team. For the body. For Christ.

If you do this, you will experience God in a new and powerful way that will transform your life. You'll be doing what Jesus does; what a Christian is supposed to do. And you won't believe how simple it is to experience more of God's love for you and for others.

Your life, and someone else's, will be far richer. What can be better than that? I think we can all bear that sort of result.

Part 2:

Getting Over It

C̲ongratulations! We've built a bridge together.
It took us several chapters to get it done, and we nearly used up all the A-words. To get this bridge constructed, we found we had to agree, accept, allow, and account. We had to avoid arrogance and assumptions. We had to bring our "A" game, wouldn't you say?

In the end, we got it done. Now, here in this brief interlude between Parts 1 and 2, we stand back, wipe away the sweat, and admire the sturdy bridge we've built.

The old saying is, "We'll cross that bridge when we come to it."

Well, we've come to it!

Just 40 miles or so from our church, you'll find a striking example of our topic. It's known as the Golden Gate Bridge. It's one of the most famous bridges in the world, and probably the area's most beloved landmark. There are longer bridges today, but I doubt any of them are quite as imposing as the Golden Gate Bridge stretching into a San Francisco fog and completely disappearing. It can be a little eerie to travel it in your car on a really misty day. You seem to be driving right into the unknown—maybe the Twilight Zone.

Sometimes, that's the way we feel when looking at a relational challenge. The bridge you and I are building doesn't connect us to Marin County, as the Golden Gate does, but to *other people*—people with whom we struggle to get along. We've learned a lot about what we need to do. We know about accepting, accommodating, and that kind of thing. But then it comes to the messy issue of living and working with difficult people. We wonder about ourselves. We wonder about the other guy. Is this "bridge" going to hold up? Are we really going to get along?

So we walk up to the bridge and tentatively take the first step onto it. Here's that moment of suspense—is the bridge going to support our weight? We try to look across, and a fog of uncertainty keeps us from seeing the other side.

I felt that way when I came to this part of the world in 1989. I was leaving a church I knew, an East Coast I knew, a way of life I knew, for a future that was built on nothing more than faith in God's plan for me. I knew he was calling me, but in 1989 I had to step out on that faith. I had to place a foot down on the first plank of a bridge to the rest of my life. They say that faith is walking to the edge of all the light you have, even before you fully understand where God is leading you.

That's what we're about to do. The first part of this book, you see, was really about other people and how we look at them. These final three chapters are about the man or woman in the mirror. We can build a bridge, but we still have to get over it—and that means getting over ourselves! In the book of Acts, we're going to find three attitudes that the early church had to uproot in order to create real fellowship, to build a bridge to a future church. We're going to do the same.

Can you handle one more bridge story?

I heard this one about a Super Bowl football game of a few years ago. I don't know whether this really happened or not, but the principle behind it is brilliant.

At halftime, the team on the losing end filed into the locker room with disgust and frustration. Nothing was working. The offense had stalled out every time it got the ball, and the defense was intimidated.

The head coach walked into the center of the room to address the team. Strangely enough, he brought a long wooden board with him, six feet long, four inches wide, two inches thick. He laid it across two benches, creating a plank bridge that was maybe two feet off the ground. The coach said, "Everybody get up and form a line at this bench." They looked at each other in bewilderment, but ultimately did what they were told. Then the coach ordered his players to climb up on the first bench, one by one, "walk the plank" from side to the next, then hop down and take a seat.

The players felt a little silly. They wondered if this was some kind of pirate thing. Were they being punished by walking the plank for their bad first half? Was this the best the coach could do for motivation?

After the exercise was completed, the coach said, "How many of you felt any fear when you walked on that four-inch-wide board from one bench to the other?"

None raised hands. A few rolled their eyes.

The coach said, "Of course not. And nobody fell off. Now what if I took this exact same board and put it out the window of a skyscraper, sixty floors from the ground, so that it led to another window six feet away? How many of you would hop up, with just as much confidence, to walk from one window to the next?"

None raised hands. There were a few wide eyes.

"So!" said the coach. "You guys walk across this board, two feet up just now, no fear at all. Put the exact same board sixty floors up, and you guys wouldn't touch it—even though you've just seen you can easily make that walk. Same feet. Same board. Same ability, right?"

He concluded, "The difference *is not physical.* It's not even the distance to the ground. It's nothing tangible at all in the real world. It's something that lives between your own ears and is very powerful. Your fear completely transforms your attitude. Did you realize fear had that kind of control over your life? What could you do on the football field *if you played without fear?"*

It's true, isn't it? The bridge isn't as formidable as we think. It's how we look at the bridge; what we know about its conditions. Our fear of falling, of failing, is a matter of faith. If we believe the promises of God, we know he wants us to walk across that gap. If there is any one thing we can always be certain God wants us to do, it's to love other people. That's an eternal absolute—you never have to spend time in prayer asking God whether or not you ought to have love for some other person. He's already laid that out, once and for all. He loved every one of us, and he wants us to love one another and settle our differences in a godly, appropriate way.

So can we make the walk? Will God give us love? Is there anything he cannot do when it is his will?

It's a no-brainer. We can build a bridge, and we can get over it. Forget the fog. Let's start walking. This is a golden gate bridge out of the fog of toxic and dysfunctional relationships, and into true joy. What lies on the other side is a reward well worth the journey.

8.

Get Over Your Fear: God Calls You Forward

H ave you ever watched with your family that classic film, "The Wizard of Oz?"

It never fails; we're always surprised in that moment when Dorothy steps out of her house, holding her dog. The entire building has just been carried through the air in some kind of crazy cyclone, and she has watched a cast of characters from her past life whizzing by the window.

But all of that has been in black and white. Remember? As soon as Dorothy steps out of that door, what does she find? The movie is now in candy-bright Technicolor. We almost squint in surprise, even though we know it's coming. Nothing around Dorothy looks like the flat farmland she has come from. She has that little terrier cradled in her arms, and I bet you remember what she says to the dog: "Toto, we're not in Kansas anymore."

That's an understatement!

Have you ever experienced a Dorothy moment? You feel as if suddenly nothing around you is the same, that everything from your past life has been picked up by some kind of whirlwind. Now you look around and long for your own version of Kansas; whatever your past has been all about. Now remember, Dorothy has spent the story up until now longing for a more exciting life. She needs to learn that we must be careful what we wish for.

The truth is that most of us actually want change and newness—but we want it to be a new, improved version of what we already have. We don't want anything that forces us to change personally. If you've got an iPod that holds 10,000 songs, you want one that holds 20,000 songs—not an entirely different kind of music device that would force you to replace your entire library. Convenient change is what we want. Problem is that change is often anything but convenient.

And that's a good thing. If we always had it our way, we'd still be riding souped-up horses to work in the morning, listening to drive-time music with specially mounted gramophones that we'd wind up with a crank. We'd be communicating by state-of-the-art telegraph. We'd be making business trips by the latest in hot air balloon technology.

Can you remember the first time you ever used a computer? (I realize some of you may not have gotten there yet!) Can you remember the fear and discomfort of learning something completely new, or perhaps how you resented being forced to do it? A lot of people held out as long as they could before succumbing to the Information Age, and now you can't get them off the Internet. They can't imagine life without it. Some people were angry at the very idea of a newfangled microwave oven, and now you couldn't take it away from them.

We know that. Even so, tomorrow will bring something new, something just as threatening to the old way of life. The only thing in daily life that doesn't change is the principle of change. The only certainty is uncertainty.

One of the first people who caught on about this modern fact of life was a man named Alvin Toffler. Back in 1970 he

wrote a book called *Future Shock*. His short-version defini-
tion of future shock was "too much change in too short a
period." He predicted the advent of a time when the acceler-
ation of new things and ideas would prove to be emotionally
disturbing to society. There would be "information over-
load," and people wouldn't be able to handle it.

I think that's right where we are. And I think that in our
discussion about building bridges to people, we're reacting
against change in the same way. Your personal world is probably far more diverse than the world of your parents. You are
surrounded by people of different ethnicity, different religions, different world views and lifestyles—and you finally
cry out those three letters: "TMI!" which stands for "Too
much information!"

We're not in Kansas anymore. Things are very different
than they used to be, and what we feel most of all is *fear*.

Growth Requires Change

If you're a parent, I want you to stop and enjoy a very
pleasant memory: the moment when you held your baby for
the first time. Can you remember how that felt? The awesome
experience of a miracle in the palm of your hands?

The face is a little squinched up, the skin remarkably
smooth, and at times the little creature seems very angry. But
you've never seen anything more beautiful in your whole
life. Can you recall just how tiny that baby seemed? You
read all the books, you did all your homework, and you still
couldn't believe just how small this new family member
was. There was that whole miracle of life, the fact that God
had given light and breath and a little voice to this infant,
and even specially prepared Mother to provide nourishment.
God didn't just have a plan, he had a beautiful and breathtaking plan for showing us this miracle of life.

I surely do remember holding my little ones, taking them home in those tiny bundles, and hearing the nurse say, "Keep that blanket tight, because it reminds them of the womb."

I took that nurse seriously, and at home I was always checking to make sure that blanket was snug and comfortable and womblike. There were days when I would fall asleep on the sofa holding my baby on my chest. My wife took pictures of me in the exact same position with each of my newborn kids on my chest. They're asleep, I'm asleep, and my adoring wife can't resist the urge to grab her camera and capture the moment on film.

Then our children began to grow. We simply provided food, milk, and love. Growth came all on its own. There was never that moment when we sat down and said, "Okay, now let's make our child grow. He needs three more pounds this month." Nature provides that part; we just sit back and enjoy.

Sometimes, growth is a little threatening! Years ago, I heard my daughter Alicia and my wife Meredith arguing downstairs in our home. They were fighting over who was taller. Meredith had once carried Alicia inside her for nine months, and now Alicia was about to be taller than the mother who brought her into this world.

I came downstairs when I heard the dispute going on, grabbed a pencil, and lined the two of them up against the wall—again, something you've probably done in your own family. Lo and behold, our daughter had taken the lead, and she was quite proud of the fact: tallest female in the Sheppard family. Meredith just scowled at her, and I got a big laugh out of the whole thing—until shortly afterwards, when our son got *his* growth spurt. Suddenly I was fighting to retain my title as the tallest male in the family. And eventually I was forced to accept the fact that I've lost the title to my son.

But what can I do? Growth is normative, as long as basic needs are met. If we continue to live, we continue to change and to grow. That child is never for a moment the same. Sometimes it seems as if you hardly get your son home from the barber before he needs another haircut.

Most of us don't realize how our bodies are in perpetual motion, all our tiny little cells dying and regenerating every second. There's no such thing as "still life." To live is to be constantly transforming toward a new creature. During the next moment, every cell of your body will be different than it was the moment that preceded it. Life is change. Life is movement. The second you stop changing, you are no longer living, and someone will be planning your funeral.

Physical growth takes care of itself. But there are other kinds of growth—mental, emotional, spiritual—that do not. They demand our cooperation and accommodation. We have to become part of the process of change.

You had to grow with the increasing demands of each year of your education. You had to grow socially and learn how to play well with others, on the playground and eventually in the home and office. You had to learn how to manage your emotions—as a baby, you'd just let 'em rip, having a tantrum when you weren't getting what you wanted. Over time, you had to manage those feelings, or risk being known as a very childish adult.

Life forces us to grow up to get along. Notice that the same is true of institutions. Does a church have growth issues? Yes it does. How about a home or a business? Absolutely.

The book of Acts is like a series of marks behind the family room door, showing the steady growth of the church—which is, indeed, the body of Christ—from infancy to maturity. Acts 2, for example, shows how the church, in its first days, had the exuberance and energy of youth. The gospel was preached, there was joy, there was the rapid growth that all children experience. The church grew enough to take in someone like Saul, its greatest enemy, who had been harassing it with vehemence.

Now that's what I call change. Let's find out how the body of Christ faced one of its first big questions.

Everyone Must Change

Yes, the church had to open its doors and let in Public Enemy Number One, a fierce persecutor who had called himself Saul. Now he claimed to have a new name and a new policy. Could he be trusted?

It was a pretty good question. The whole existence of Christianity had offended everything the old Saul believed. The Jesus movement was a weed infestation in the garden of the Hebrew faith, and Saul was a passionate gardener who was pulling weeds right and left. Then, on a trip to Damascus where he intended to uproot another infestation of Christians, God headed him off at the pass. You may have heard about the Damascus Road experience. If Paul's name changed by one letter, his life changed in every way possible. It was turned inside out. Suddenly he had fallen from his horse, a light blinded his eyes, and Jesus was speaking. He said, "I am not the enemy. The enemy is in your mirror, because of what your own sin does to you. You've been fighting the only cure."

Think about the worst, most objectionable person you can imagine—someone who stands for everything you loathe. What would happen if you discovered, in the space of one moment, that you had to devote yourself to worshiping and serving that person? That was required of Paul, all in the space of one moment. He had to wrap his mind around an entire alternate universe.

Growth requires change, but rarely that radical. Jesus wanted to do fantastic, unique things through Paul, so the transformation had to be just that dramatic. Paul would be as effective as he was only because his testimony was so compelling, so dramatic.

Here is how it was happening. This new movement called The Way was made up of Jewish believers who had come to see that Jesus was indeed the long-awaited Messiah. But God's plan was a little bigger than they had imagined, and both their hearts and minds would have to expand in order to embrace an unexpected reality.

God needed a Hebrew scholar of the Law par excellence to receive the revelation that non-Jews would also be invited to follow Christ. He also needed someone with impeccable credentials, Roman citizenship (a kind of passport for the empire), flawless understanding of Greek culture, a deep philosophical bent, and a commanding leadership presence. That's who Saul was. He was the change agent God needed.

But to become that agent, Saul himself needed to change. God first blinded him, so that he would be helpless and dependent upon the Christian worker sent to assist him. It was a man named Ananias whom God sent to find Saul in a house on Straight Street.

And notice that it took great courage for Ananias to obey what God told him to do. Acts 9:13 tells us that he said, in effect, "Whatever you say, Lord, but I don't like the things I've heard about this Saul dude. I know for a fact he's in town to stir up trouble with people who love you—and you want me to go lay hands on him and heal him?"

That's just what the Lord wanted. We don't always understand what God is up to, but that's all right. He does.

Have you ever felt the need to be obedient to God in a way that seemed to make no rational sense? Perhaps you've awakened in the middle of the night and felt the impulse to pray for someone. You couldn't understand why, but you just felt this compulsion: "Pray for your cousin John, right now!" Many people would call it crazy, because there's been no phone call, no letter, no news of any kind to prompt that impression—just this sense, or a still small voice, urging us to pray. Then within days or weeks you found out there was good reason to be obedient to the prompting of the Spirit.

But what if God were calling you to do something a little more costly? What if you really concluded that he wants you to enroll in a graduate school to prepare for a career change, or perhaps move to another city or country to serve him there? You can bet that your loved ones would be all over you about that. They'd say, "Are you sure you know what you're doing?" And they'd be right to check out and discern whether or not this "leading" is indeed from the Lord. We need a number of "check points" for verifying God's call upon us for the really big moves in life. We need to seek wise counsel. We need to pray deeply, and we need to make sure that what we intend to do is in conformity to God's will.

Even so, there are times when we just know God wants us to do something, and it's something that the world's conventional wisdom would never advise.

Do you have the courage to do what Ananias did?

By the way, it's worth noting that there is another Ananias mentioned in Acts. He, along with his wife Sapphira, was struck down because they lied to Peter and, in fact, to God about their giving. They are famous because of their disobedience. But thankfully, the other Ananias is famous for just the opposite, and his obedience helped Saul begin his journey of spiritual transformation.

Fearless Followers

Now what if Saul had listened to some of the men in his entourage after that light hit him on the way to Damascus? Don't you just imagine there were a few friends who said, "Saul, my man, take some time to think this over. Heat stroke makes us see and believe wacky things! Let's get a good night's sleep, maybe arrest a few Christians, and I'm sure you'll be feeling much better in no time."

Or what if Saul had been obedient, but Ananias said, "No way would God tell me to visit that sadistic hate-monger named Saul. I took an extra look through the Scriptures here, and David, Gideon, Samson, all those guys wiped out the enemies of God; they didn't *help* them."

The truth is, we think too much. We rationalize too much. Now, I'm not saying we shouldn't use the good brains God gave us. The problems come when we use them to explain away the simple truth that God is trying to provide us. His kingdom is blessed in magnificent ways when ordinary people practice simple obedience, regardless of their fear.

If you could see the map of your life from the heavenly perspective right now, what surprises would you witness? There would be so many! If you could see your whole life on this earth mapped out, birth to death, past to future, you would see that he wants to do wonderful things in you and through you. The only requirement is that you follow him fearlessly; that you trust him in obedience, walking out to the edge of all the light that you have, even when you don't fully understand where he's taking you.

That's one of the toughest steps on the bridge, isn't it? We have fear of other people. Saul was just as apprehensive about the Christians as they were about him, but God was building a bridge between them. Why? So that he could build a bridge between the cross and all the people of the world. By the way, if you could see that map of your life from the heavenly perspective, my prediction is that this would be the theme of it. God's will for us is always about people. It's always about bridge-building. It's always about the Great Commission and the Great Commandment, about helping other people learn who he is and how much he loves them.

His will for you may be to become a recording artist or a restaurant owner or a business person of some specific kind;

that's just the detail part. The big picture is that he wants to use your life to bring other lives into his kingdom.

When that Ananias moment comes ("Lord, it's too dangerous!") or that Saul of Tarsus moment ("Lord, it's too crazy!"), are you going to say what's really on your mind ("Lord, I'm afraid!")? That's a start. It's okay to tell him that this feels scary. It's okay to tell him that you don't feel emotionally prepared to walk into what I once heard a speaker call "the zone of the unknown." But don't reason yourself out of God's business. Obey him anyhow.

Remember what David wrote: "Yea, though I walk through the valley of the shadow of death, I will fear no evil, for thou art with me." David had to change, too. He had to make the transition from pasture to palace, from shepherd to king. And the transition was anything but simple because had to deal with the hatred and jealousy of current king, Saul, who was trying to have him killed. David had to hide out in caves for years as he awaited divine intervention. It must have seemed that God had forgotten his promise. Yet David said to God, "I can do this, for you are here with me." Somehow the fear flees when we feel his hand in ours. Not only will he hold your hand; not only will he walk with you. He will lead you through that valley. All you have to do is follow—fearlessly.

Wherever He Leads

I wonder where he is leading you right now. I wonder what people issues are in your life, what bridges remain half-built, needing that renewed commitment to finish the good work he has begun.

The key to getting through this period of change is knowing who we are and settling into God's leadership. Saul became Paul, but he learned something about himself that was much deeper than a name change. Listen to the words he wrote to the Romans:

> *Those who are led by the Spirit of God are sons of God. For you did not receive a spirit that makes you a slave again to fear, but you received the Spirit of sonship. And by him we cry, "Abba, Father." The Spirit himself testifies with our spirit that we are God's children. Now if we are children, then we are heirs—heirs of God and co-heirs with Christ, if indeed we share in his sufferings in order that we may also share in his glory.*
>
> *(Romans 8:14-17)*

Fear is human nature, but it's not godly nature. We all experience it, but we overcome it when we realize who is on our side. *We are sons of God!* Do you really believe that? If you believe it, it will change the way you live—totally. Moses once sent spies into Canaan. Most of them came back and said, "We're like grasshoppers compared to the guys who hang out in that country. They will step on us. But Joshua and Caleb said, "It's not true! We are sons of God. We are the children of one who parted the Red Sea, who fed us with bread from the skies. Where's this fear coming from?"

In those verses from Romans, Paul says that the key is the Holy Spirit, the one who whispers to us what we need to do. And as he does so, he "testifies with our spirit" that we are God's children, that we have kingdom privileges, and as a matter of fact, that we are "co-heirs with Christ." Can you imagine that? Co-heirs with the only Son of God! And since, as Paul explains in Romans, we were crucified with him—our sins nailed to that cross—we "may also share in his glory."

Don't you feel a little fear melting away already? Sharing in God's glory means being a part of all the magnificent things that Christ wants to do in this world. Before Damascus, Saul was a prominent Jewish man, a rising star in temple circles. He was well-educated, someone who was going places. But he would have faded into the mists of time if he hadn't crawled up out of the dust of that road and said, "Yes, Jesus. I will do just as you say." As a result, he shared in Christ's glory. He was a key mover in the exciting early years of the Christian movement.

We have the benefit of these stories of Acts, and those letters he wrote years later, as a wise and mature believer who knew that what didn't make sense in the beginning was golden in retrospect. That's the way it is with your life. He will call you out of your comfort zone, call you to do something that not many people in your life can understand, and it won't seem to make any worldly sense. But if you hear God's call clearly and follow it obediently, someday you'll be on your knees saying, "Thank you, Lord!"

You'll be so much farther up the road, and you'll have some of the answers, but you'll know that change was required to get where you are now. Discomfort was required. Stubborn focus on the will of God was required, and perhaps a considerable measure of personal sacrifice. Whatever you lay before that altar, however—whether it's lost friends, forfeited financial security, whatever it may be—if you're truly going where God wants you to go, you can always be certain that the rewards shine brightly enough to make the sacrifices look miniscule.

For right now, God wants you to stop focusing on fear and look instead at who is calling you forward.

The Fear of the Lord

I'd be remiss if I didn't mention one healthy kind of fear. It's one that God's people once used all the time, and are now hesitant to mention. What do you think about the "fear of the Lord?"

We have to use that phrase with a careful disclaimer, but we can't ignore it. Some people hear the words "fear of the Lord" and they think of God with a lightning bolt in one hand, boiling over with anger and preparing to punish us for something. Of course we want those people to know the wonderful, affectionate God of love, the God of forgiveness. But the Bible does teach that we should be, in the King James Version language, "God-fearing men and women." In the old language, that word was a bit more synonymous with respect, with a humble and worshipful approach to God. But the word *respect* doesn't quite say it, does it? We used to use the word "awe," as in "Our God is an awesome God." But that word has been messed up, too. Now we use *awesome* to describe pizza or the latest tune on the radio.

What I'm getting at here is that we serve a powerful, magnificent, infinite God whose glory is so intense that it would devour us to look upon it directly. We need to worship that God with a deep love, respect, awe, and yes, even fear— not so much fear that he will strike us down if we are disobedient, but fear of what life would be like if we wandered away from him.

You see, in our generation we've reacted against those days when our grandparents overdid the "wrath of God" and underdid the love of God. We scared people away from the church by making non-believers think God was basically angry all the time, and that he was all about punishment. We were right to get away from that, but instead we've substituted a God so non-fearsome that he's more like a happy, un-demanding friend we may or may not call upon. And if he wants us to do something, well, we'll think about it. We'll get back to ya on that, God.

The unobtrusive "big buddy" God is just as mistaken a view as the lightning-hurling one. The real God is indeed loving, but also awesome, mighty, infinite, sovereign, and holy. And if we say no to him, we should be very afraid of what we will do to our own lives. It's not that he lives to punish us. It's more like, as C. S. Lewis once said, God spends all our lives trying to help us say, "Have it your way, Lord"—because he knows it will bring us true fulfillment. If we continue to refuse, however, God will eventually say to us, "Okay, then you must have it *your* way." And our way is what we should fear. Because only his way works. There is nothing in the universe apart from our God and his will that can do anything but ultimately make us miserable.

We need a healthy "fear" (respect, worshipful comprehension) of God, and a healthy fear of life outside the safety of his arms.

I Hear You Knockin' But You Can't Come In

Change can be frightening, but it can also be threatening.

Let's return to the story of Paul, still in Acts 9. Ananias was obedient to God, going to the blinded Saul, laying hands on him, healing him, and beginning the process of discipling a new Christian. Paul began to declare that Jesus was Christ, the Messiah. People in that town could see that a miracle had happened. Indeed, this man had been blind spiritually just as he was, for a brief while, blind physically—and now he could see. He was even preaching in the synagogues, defeating the arguments of his old associates by proving Jesus was the Messiah. As a matter of fact, now *he* was the first name on the death list. For the first time, Paul's eloquence got him in hot water, and the Christians had to sneak him out of town in a basket by night.

But all this was in Damascus, not Jerusalem. When Paul returned to the big city to meet the disciples there, it was a different story. They hadn't witnessed any of this road-to-

Damascus drama. They hadn't heard any of those presentations in the synagogues. All they knew was that, in Jerusalem, this was the same man who held people's coats while they stoned Stephen, the bold young believer, to death. This was the Big Bad Wolf at their door, and they were supposed to believe his line about being converted? Not on their lives! They were smarter than that.

We might speculate that God was whispering to those disciples, telling them to walk to the door in faith and open it up. But their fear was shouting much louder. They didn't want any part of Saul, or Paul, or Y'all, or a visitor by any other name with this one's track record.

And it's here that a wonderful name comes into the story. He has been mentioned once in Acts 4, but now he is going to become a central figure in Paul's life. His name is Barnabas, and we associate him with encouragement. Wherever he's found in the New Testament, he is bringing people together, knocking down walls, building bridges between folks, spurring people toward their best in Christ.

Can't you envision how highly charged this situation was? How emotions were running rampant? The disciples thought that trickery was afoot. Paul only knew that the Christians on the other side of that door had been there when Stephen was martyred. They had seen him at his very worst, and now they might kill him just as the Jewish leaders in Damascus had tried to do. The disciples didn't want to open the door, and Paul wasn't completely certain he wanted it opened.

There must have been shouting, arguing, threats. Barnabas, however, was a quiet man compared to the likes of Peter and Paul, the two who were on opposite sides of the wall. We can always use a few quiet people in our churches, offices, and families, can't we? We need people who can be calm and unemotional, discerning the voice and the will of God, when fear and bitterness are shouting over everything.

The others could only perceive a threat. Barnabas perceived the voice of God, saying, "I'll vouch for this one. Open the door."

Again, we've reached a crisis point. God's plan for global Christianity hangs in the balance here, but nobody cares about that for the moment. Everybody is trying to hurry back to their comfort zones, but there is always one individual who stands in the gap, who bridges the two parties and helps them get over their mutual fear.

Oh, how we all need a Barnabas from time to time. When we feel fear, we often need a Barnabas. When we feel threatened, we need that quiet voice of reason. When we wonder about God's will in a confusing situation, we need that wise, positive encourager who pushes us toward our best and even says, "Hey, I'll go with you." And sometimes we ourselves have to be a Barnabas to someone else.

Hasn't God already raised up a Barnabas or two in your life? If you haven't recognized them yet, you will, just as sure as you commit to stepping out in faith and building the bridges God has called you to build and cross.

Bridging the Gap

Believe it or not, even the Apostle Pauls of the world need a Barnabas. I'm not talking about the brand-new believer Paul here, who needs an advocate just to get into the meeting room.

I'm talking about later on, in Acts 15, when Paul had progressed to the point of arranging mission trips. At this point, he's gone on one of them and it was successful. Paul is gaining his confidence by this time, and no one is questioning his sincerity as a Christian. He's gone out there and risked his life, preached the Word, won souls, and work miracles. So now it's time for him to start packing for a second missionary journey. His steady companion, of course, is the same Barnabas that sponsored him in that tense Jerusalem moment. Paul says, "So! Where will we go this time?"

Barnabas says, "Tell you what, I'll go get John Mark and we'll put our heads together."

Paul stops and turns toward Barnabas. "I hope you didn't just say John Mark."

"Sure," says Barney, "Why not?"

"Because he bailed on us last time, that's why not! Don't you remember how he couldn't handle it when things got tough, and he cleared out and went running home to Mama? This is God's work, and it's not for the weak."

Paul had a point. John Mark was a young man who'd been around the disciples since he was a kid, when JM's mother hosted a congregation in her home. He'd signed up for the trip—only to discover he had bit off more than he could chew. Remember, these weren't board-sponsored mission trips where you climb onto a plane, meet some friendly local children, tell them a Bible story, then enjoy a day at the beach before going home. This was the kind of mission trip where mobs come out with big rocks in their hands and curses on their tongues. This was the kind of mission trip where sometimes people don't make the return trip. So Paul was not in the mood to take this previously unreliable spiritual soldier behind enemy lines again.

But Barnabas, quiet as he was, knew when to hold the line. He said, "I think you're wrong about John Mark. He wants another chance, and our God is about second chances—particularly for this second trip."

Paul knew when to hold the line, too. So they argued back and forth and couldn't come to an agreement. It's a little sad, isn't it? Barnabas vouching for someone again, someone who had once done the wrong thing. It should have reminded Paul of someone. It should have made him think about the grace he would write about in so many of

175

Moses didn't look upon it like that. He got beyond the fear of his own finish line, and poured himself into the training of his successor—the final test of a real leader. The ultimate service we provide for God is to decrease that others may increase. Many a track athlete has run his race to perfection, only to stumble when it was time to pass the baton.

Yet even so, our God is good. In the case of Paul, Barnabas, and John Mark, the result of the dispute was multiplication by division. Paul went one way, the other two traveled in another direction, and God used all of it. There are times when we fail to build the bridge, but God builds it right on top of us.

Keep following him. Go from fear to faith, building bridges from one impossible goal to the next. In the Lord, we have nothing to fear but fear itself.

9.

Get Over Your Pride: God Wants More for You

O kay, I'm going to get personal with you. I figure we've made it through eight chapters together, so maybe I've earned the right to poke around a little bit in your life. Or at least in your closet.

That's what I'm getting at. I want to know what's in your closet.

I'm talking about the one in your bedroom, where your wardrobe lives. I imagine you could learn a lot about people by studying the clothing items they keep around—particularly those items that are pushed over to the side, the "low-traffic" areas of the closet. Don't you have a few of those things you know you won't be wearing anytime soon?

Here comes the touchy part. It just could be there are a few items in your closet that are actually no longer, let's say, in conformance to your physical contours anymore. Do you have a problem throwing those out or giving them away? I know – you figure you *might* lose the necessary pounds. It could happen. Who knows, you might even survive a plane crash, live for four years on an island just like Tom Hanks, and come back home buff and able to wear those old clothes again. Then you could tell your spouse, "I told you I needed to save these slacks! If I would've listened to you, we'd have given them to Goodwill!"

The truth is that time passes and we change. As we observed in the preceding chapter, being alive means moving on—in many ways. The times themselves change, meaning that fashions come and go. But we also change. Sometimes we gain weight as we move into our middle years, or we may become smaller as we go into our later years.

Perhaps we find it difficult to let go of those clothing items because of the symbolism. Do you know what I'm talking about? You can no longer fit into those pants, but if you discard them, you're admitting you're not the size you once were. Of course, an eating plan and regular exercise may be nowhere on your immediate agenda—but still. You can't pull the trigger on moving on with your wardrobe. That's why a lot of us have some funny things in our closet.

We tell ourselves that we're being sentimental, but in reality, you know what it is? Pride. We can't quite admit to ourselves that we're growing older. We can't come to terms with the fact that our bodies are changing. As a matter of fact, some of us even try wearing those clothes that are a little too tight. And when we do, we run the risk of tempting a friend to walk up to us and say, "I love you, but you look...special, and not in a good way. I know yours is the kind of personality that likes to let it all hang out in life, but when it comes to this outfit, you need to push some of it back in!"

Of course, some of your friends would never say that to you, because they wouldn't want to hurt your pride.

There's the word. That's such a crucial issue for many of us—*pride*. Have you ever thought about its impact on your actions and decisions? There are so many things God wants from us and for us, and pride often keeps them from happening.

The early church certainly had to face this issue. Let's find out more about that.

Up on the Roof

We took a look at Acts 9 in the last chapter, and we learned about Paul and the other disciples. Fear was the great obstacle in that situation, particularly fear of someone who had a bad record but tremendous potential. Everybody had to be courageous to experience the incredible things that God had in store.

In the next chapter, Acts 10, we meet a man named Cornelius. There's not a great deal of background about this man in the Bible. We'd love to know more about Cornelius, because we have questions about him: How did this pagan from far away, this Roman centurion, come to be a "God-fearing man"? Most of the Romans, of course, brought with them their own religion—or lack thereof.

Yet even in the gospels we occasionally encounter Roman soldiers who served the true God. Our Lord was at work in that time of colliding cultures, you see. The Mediterranean world had become an open marketplace of ideas, of languages, of religions. Was that a threat to God's people? No, it was an open door! It was a whole new world of opportunity. We see it so clearly in the New Testament, and if only we could see that same thing in our own diverse world.

God sent his Son at the precise timing he did because the world was finally opening up. The Romans were building roads. The Greeks were providing a one-size-fits-all language. Ships were sailing, importing and exporting ideas as well as goods. More people could read and write, and share their documents from city to city.

What about today? What about satellite communication? Internet connectivity? Should Christians be afraid of these things, or do you think God has his own plans to use them for his kingdom?

Cornelius was a Roman who commanded 100 other men (the official charge of a centurion). He had abandoned pagan gods for the God of the Jewish people, and he reflected this in daily prayer, in offerings, and in helping the poor. That's what Luke, the author of Acts, tells us. Now he was not a Jew just by worshiping the right God; he wouldn't have been circumcised, and he wouldn't have followed every ancient tradition and festival. But he did, in fact, fear and serve the Lord to the extent of his knowledge.

Acts 10 tells us about a vision he had one day. Luke, who provides many significant details in his accounts, tells us that it came precisely at three o'clock in the afternoon. There was an angel of the Lord, and the angel began by affirming the Roman's good works, which were pleasing to God. Then he gave Cornelius a task: send for a man named Simon Peter who will be found at the home of Simon the Tanner by the ocean in Joppa.

And just like that, the vision was over. Cornelius began to tell the others in his home about it, and he sent two servants and his personal attendant on journey to find Peter.

At lunchtime the next day, we're told that Peter climbed up to the roof to pray. This was common in that part of the world. People kept ladders for climbing to the roof, and they could sit on a thatch of hay or straw and enjoy moments of solitude. Apparently Peter had a little experience that you've probably had: his stomach began to growl! He was at prayer, and the spirit was willing but the flesh was preoccupied with the desire to eat. It was noon, right? Perhaps he could smell the kitchen aromas wafting up from downstairs, and he kept seeing a big, juicy meal in his mind. I grew up in a church that usually had big meals after Sunday worship services, and I guarantee you there were many days when we could hardly wait for the benediction because of the aromas coming from the dining hall.

Yet in Peter's case, his natural inclination to eat was interrupted by a vision. In this vision, there was a large sheet that seemed to come down from heaven. Picnic! No problem there. But when it got down to eye level, he saw all kinds of animals that weren't supposed to be there. He looked at the birds, the mammals, even a few reptiles, and thought, "This is so wrong." Maybe there was big rasher of bacon sizzling away. To Peter, that was the devil's breakfast! Maybe he thought he knew this drill. He would be tempted to eat, but he would impress the Lord by holding out for the kosher burgers they were grilling downstairs. Peter was a proud observer of Jewish traditions. A man who gets through his whole life without ever eating any forbidden food is going to have a little pride of accomplishment, right?

Then, according to Acts 10, a heavenly voice instructs him to go ahead and chow down!

Peter instinctively knew this was from God, and not Satan. Still, he replied, "Yeah, right!"

The voice spoke again: "No joke. Smorgasbord. Dig in!" (Or words to that effect. You'll notice I have my own private paraphrase of these holy conversations.)

Peter said, "You're not getting it. If I eat this stuff, a little buzzer will go off somewhere, and my colleagues will be all over me. Where I come from, these foods are off limits; verboten; taboo. It's somewhere in Deuteronomy. You could look it up."

But the voice repeated the same command. "Dig in."

Just about now, Peter may have been thinking back to his midnight snack from the night before. After all, this was an awfully crazy dream to be having on a rooftop in the middle of the day.

Then again, this is Peter we're talking about. Some of the strangest stories about Jesus involved Peter. He was invited by Jesus to step out of a boat in deep water in the middle of a storm, and he was brave enough to do it. Later, after insisting that he would never forsake Jesus, it for only a matter of hours before he swore that he never even met the man. Yet on the day of Pentecost, who did the Holy Spirit select to preach the good news to persons from far and near? Peter!

So Christ had already summoned Peter on some incredible journeys. But this one took the cake, so to speak.

He realized this was another "step out of the boat" moment. *Step out of the paradigm; step out of the old habit. Leave the pride of tradition behind. God is trying to teach you something.* And by now, I think you know where we're going with this.

The Few, the Proud

This much I've learned about God: He never drops by your house to say, "Hey, I've got this new idea I'm thinking about. Wanted your opinion."

He loves us, but he knows better than to let us in on his plans. We would be about 100 percent likely to mess up any godly endeavor for which we had comprehensive advance information. When God moves, we never the full scope of his activity until we've responded in obedience to the first set of commands. Have you ever noticed that? This is why he didn't send Peter a training DVD, telling him that non-kosher foods were now officially on the acceptable menu. He waited until the right moment and found a teaching strategy that Peter was never likely to forget. He had to do this because Peter was both spiritual and stubborn, and it was going to be difficult to guide him away from a lifetime of training and tradition—and pride.

Before we have a good laugh at Peter's expense, we need to ask ourselves if we could be a little guilty of the same kind of pride. You see, we all have a way of getting the habits of life into certain grooves. We might say that we wear paths into the daily landscape of our lives. I'm sure you've seen a patch of woods where people have cut through in one place over the years, just to get somewhere faster. Grass no longer grows in that path, because too many feet have trod along it. We have all kinds of paths or grooves—restaurants we like to frequent on Friday nights; things we like to do on Sunday afternoon; a certain order of what features we read first in a magazine. These things aren't good or bad, but just life and the way we grow accustomed to living it.

But sometimes we have well-worn grooves and God looks at them and call them *ruts*. Ruts are places where nothing grows anymore—including us. Traditions can be great, but if become more committed to them than we ought, they will cut off our spiritual circulation and stop the flow of the Spirit's movement in some area of our lives where growth requires change.

Think about Peter up on that rooftop. Do you really think it was sheer spiritual obedience that made him disdain the food that was offered? No, because he had the voice of God telling him he had divine permission. Dietary habits were a well-worn groove for Peter. Up to that moment, there had been nothing wrong with that groove. But now God was proclaiming it a rut. He wanted Peter to understand that what had been a good tradition for the past would be a stifling one for the future.

Until now, traditions and holidays and diets were a way of creating symbols for holiness, external evidences of being set apart unto God. But now it was time to break down some barriers and dividing walls; Jesus was for everyone who repented of sin and trusted him for salvation. Diets and circumcision would soon prove to be obstacles, not measurements of holiness.

What are some of the well-worn grooves of our time? Dietary restrictions are definitely not one of them! I've been to more than a few church barbecues. But we have other areas, don't we? In previous chapters we discussed music, one of the great church disputes of these last few decades. Over the centuries, the praise music has changed to reflect its time, to help us reach new people through the culture they understand. But we wear those paths into dust. The grooves become ruts, and eventually things are lifeless. If you had a Peter-like vision today, perhaps that sheet would come down from heaven with instrumentalists and song leaders standing on it, playing music that would appeal to people whose taste is radically different than your own. Indeed, you may be inclined to say, "Surely not, Lord! We've never had that music in our church before, and we're not about to start now!"

And I wouldn't be a bit surprised if God said to you, "I'm the author of the whole tonal scale. I created every key, every note, every sound the ear can hear. And I don't make junk. Sing these new songs with the same joy you have in your heart when they strike up your favorite song."

God is always on the move. Please understand me clearly. He never changes. He is the same yesterday, today, and forever. But people do. Jesus described the gospel as new wine, and he talked about the importance of changing the wineskins to accommodate it. You see, they would make a bag out of the skin of a goat or some animal, and it would hold wine. As the wine fermented, pressure would build and it would stretch the skin. The new, unfermented wine would cause it to break, and you'd be cleaning wine stains off the floor. We've found out that some of the old musical wineskins don't express the praises of God as well for some believers as they do for others. So unless we're willing to separate truth from tradition and method from message, we risk losing the refreshing wine of God's manifested presence in our midst.

When I was coming along as a new Christian, the Sunday School hour was a time when people got together in their groups and learned about the Bible. Most churches found it to be an effective, convenient method of teaching children and adults alike the Word of God. Sunday school was where it was happening, and it was a whole culture unto itself. Nowadays, some church leaders have noticed that home groups, meetings in people's living rooms or on their backyard decks, really seems to get a more effective, convenient way of getting the job done. We still have those Sunday morning classes in many places, but there's been a huge movement for home Bible study and fellowship. And sure enough, that violates the groove some people have been in; that's not the way Dad and Granddad did it! Yet if you study your history, you'll find that the Sunday school never existed until a century or so ago—and the early church did their thing mostly in people's homes. One is not better than the other; it's a matter of our willingness to leave our pride behind and go with the Holy Spirit, who moves where he will.

The teaching of truth must never change in the church, but the methods, strategies, and systems for disseminating that truth will, at times, have to change. Some of us have a hard time with that, because we have our favorite old wineskins that we've been carrying around for decades. We have ideas about how things are supposed to be done, and we might resist changing them not because of holiness issues, but—if we're really honest—simple, stubborn pride or personal familiarity. We need to separate the living wine of the gospel from the old, dead goat skin that is simply the container.

Groove Busters

God wants more from you. He's not content for you to rest in your ruts, because he knows how much happier, more energized, you are when you're growing and learning new things. He knows that your effectiveness in serving the kingdom is nearly non-existent when you're beating the same everyday path from Point A to Point B to Point C and back. He's always trying to build new bridges—always throwing up little "detour" signs to force us out our trances and make us think about how things *could* be.

He wants to take us to new places, but that's going to mean change in our lives. And sometimes, that's going to threaten our pride, because we like to think we already had all the answers. It was humbling for me when I left Philadelphia to come to California. Just about every little detail of my world, other than my family, had to change. For one thing, Philly culture and West Coast culture are like night and day—just very different. I could write a book about the differences between the old community and the new one. I was asking God, "Are you sure you got the right guy for this? It's a big state out here! There's got to be a California pastor who would be five times as effective as me in this setting."

I had no idea where God was going to lead me. He didn't send me the training DVD or any travel brochures. He sprung it on me just like he did Peter. All I had was a vision of a growing church that was reaching the lost with the gospel and teaching them to become fully devoted followers of Christ. Part of the vision was to launch a radio ministry, and I had a few other ideas about what my future might look like. In the 1980s, I used to share these ideas with friends. The vision had a number of components, but it had no address. I didn't know where the church would be, or what it would look like.

You see, God gave me only the pieces of information I needed. He didn't give me too many details because, like Peter, I wouldn't have been able to comprehend everything God was going to do.

When the time came, my "sheet descending from heaven" was the idea of diversity. I have always loved diversity, but I had settled into the groove of ministering to all-black churches. It was simply a paradigm I accepted without question. As I mentioned earlier, most churches in America are not very ethnically diverse. Sometimes that's due to the fact that the neighborhoods they're in are comprised of one predominate racial group. In fact, when I was growing up, there were parts of Philadelphia that blacks only drove through, and it simply wouldn't have occurred to our church to seek to attract folks from such neighborhoods. That wasn't part of the groove of that time.

As a matter of fact, in the late 80s, conventional wisdom suggested that the best formula for growing churches was to be intentionally homogeneous—that is, go after a specific demographic in your city or region. I traveled my well-worn path all the way across America to the Bay Area, thinking I would grow a church by utilizing this formula.

Of course, I had read that there is neither Jew nor Greek, slave nor free, male nor female, as Paul tells us in Galatians 3:28. "For you are all one in Christ." I believed it; I just hadn't been exposed to a church where generational, cultural, ethnic, and socio-economic diversity was the rule, not the exception.

So I arrived in California and began to pray, preach, and cast vision...and people stayed away in droves. Something just wasn't connecting with the vision that had brought me to the Bay Area. "Okay, Lord," I said in frustration. "I moved three thousand miles to get here. That's a long way. When are you going to bring the people?" We met in a theater with a capacity of 300, and there were about 50 people there for church. Sometimes they sat together in the center part, and in frustration I'd sometimes ask them to spread out, so it would it at least *look* like better attendance. At other times, I'd ask them to move into the center section so I didn't have to look all over the place and see all of those empty seats while I was preaching! I was confused and at times angry with God. I can remember fighting discouragement week after week, as I prepared to walk to the pulpit and bring the good news to a handful of believers.

Just seeing the church grow by the twos and fews was a victory to our members, but not to me. By my first pastoral anniversary with the church, I was downright despondent. *Where are all the people, Lord?* I loved the dozens of people we had, but I wanted to fulfill the Great Commission. There were millions of people living within our reach, and we couldn't even hit 100?

I kept praying to God, and he answered. But he did it his way, without consulting me. There started to be a trickle of people who didn't look like me. One Sunday we had two new white members, and I thought that was nice, cute even, but I didn't have a clue about what God had in store for our church. In Philadelphia, we'd had 1,000 members—999 black, and one nice white lady. She was a wonderful woman who could fit in and be joyful whether people looked like her or not. And now here I was in California with two white members. Fine.

But I began to take notice when people of all colors continued to come. By my seventh anniversary, the church had about 250 members and a full 20 percent of them were not black. It wasn't just about race, either. We were drawing people from every income bracket, from every educational level or no educational level. I don't know when it happened, but the light finally came on for me. Peter's spiritual paradigm shift happened rather quickly, but mine took years. *God is doing something here.* It had to be God. This trend had not been by design. I hadn't even thought about it. And that was just the beginning. Years later, there were thousands of people in our fellowship, and nearly half of them were not black.

When God does something all on his own, and it has nothing to do with your seminary training, or your special skills, or the goals chart you spent hours making and tacking to your office wall—only the wisdom and power of God himself—it just might humble you. You might even realize that this is the way it's always supposed to be. When things happen that can only be explained by supernatural power, then God gets all the glory.

That's a groove buster and a pride buster.

Let Us Break Bread Together

Peter's story was not over.

He did pass the first part of the test, but there's always a Part 2 when God is preparing us for something new. Have you noticed that?

It's just good teaching procedure. We do this ourselves when we train our children to swim or ride a bicycle. We start by saying, "Jump off the side of the pool, and I'll catch you." Or, "See if you can peddle this bike and keep it balanced while I walk right beside you with my hand on your back." We give a little bit of a challenge, a chance for a small victory. Then we raise the stakes a little bit, make things a little tougher. We bring the pupil along carefully.

God did this with Peter. He showed him the sheet of forbidden food just to give him the big idea, and to let him cope with the shock of the lesson by himself without having to interact with others. But now something new happens. And you and I can see it coming, because Acts 10 has already recorded how Cornelius, this godly centurion, has had his own vision and sent his men to go fetch Peter. Now comes the real test.

We've already talked about Cornelius. He had adopted the God of the Jews, and was serving him as best he could. This wasn't a test for him as much as a reward for his gifts and his prayers that have been mentioned. God isn't only about testing, you see—there are plenty of times when he seems to say, "You've really been obedient to me, and I'm well pleased. I have a nice surprise for you." The reward for Cornelius in this case is being part of a great, central story in the annals of the early church. (For that matter, it ends up being a reward for Peter and everyone else involved.)

Acts tells us that Peter is still pondering Part 1 of his mid-term exam, the meaning of the food, when God breaks into his thoughts and says, "There are some men downstairs looking for you. Go and invite them in. You're going to meet Cornelius. He's a Roman, but he's one of us. You've got my word on that."

Remember what this book is about. When God builds bridges, they always lead to people. Peter has dealt with his stomach, but now he's got to deal with the kind of people he has been taught to avoid. Not only a gentile but a Roman. Not only a Roman but a centurion! This is the kind of man who beat and spat upon Jesus. The voice of the Lord has credited this particular soldier, but it's hard to wipe out a mountain of prejudice and intense emotions in a single moment.

God works from the inside out. He changes your mind and your spirit, then he tests it out with real, flesh-and-blood people. If he's working on your proud attitude about being around poor and homeless people, sooner or later he's going to put you in a situation requiring you to be with them for the purpose of love and service. God's business isn't about talking the talk. We don't build castles in the air, but build bridges on the earth with real foundations.

Peter must be feeling nervous, but he comes down from the roof and meets the delegation, invites them in as guests, and everyone hits it off. They break bread together—the kind of thing Jesus was always being criticized for doing with "unsuitable" companions—and friendships begin to form. The next day the group sets off for the home of Cornelius. It wasn't a terribly long journey, but philosophically, it would be a vast journey for Peter or for any Jew. He is surrounded by these people he's been taught to look down upon. A Jew was considered impure and unfit for worship if his body even brushed against that of a gentile. And again, the Romans were intruders, conquerors, crucifiers. Yet Jesus forgave them from the cross as he built a bridge of forgiveness from heaven to earth. Now Peter is being called to live like Jesus. The first half of this book of Acts is all about Peter learning to do that. And the big idea is that you and I must live like Jesus, too.

God commands us to put away our pride, check egos at the door, and go to people. We shouldn't even need to wait for a delegation to come fetch us as Peter did. God took the initiative in Christ to come and fetch us. We're called to go to those who needs us and bring them the gospel. That's a journey we're always traveling, a bridge we never finish crossing.

Journey's End

When Peter arrives at the home of this Roman centurion, what do you think happens? The man bows at Peter's feet! This is a nearly miraculous display from a conquering Roman. There was a time when Peter denied on three occasions that he even knew Christ, for fear of men like this. And here is a Roman officer bowing humbly and expressing gratitude that Peter would come to his home.

Falling to his knees was very appropriate in light of what God was doing in that moment. In Philippians 2, there's a passage about the humility of Christ, who didn't insist upon his status as the Lord of the Universe, but who humbled himself and became obedient to death, "that at the name of Jesus every knee should bow, in heaven and on earth and under the earth" (Philippians 2:10). Humility is the very opposite of the pride we're discussing in this chapter. Pride is a prison that confines us within ourselves, prevents us from reaching out to others. It keeps the wonderful journey from ever happening. But when two people from very different backgrounds are united in Christ, a little bit of Philippians 2 happens. We humble ourselves in imitation and obedience to Christ, we experience him profoundly, and we kneel in worship of the One who made it possible.

Peter, who is somewhat embarrassed by this act of humility, tells Cornelius to get up. "I am only a man," he says. The two men go inside the home, where a large gathering of people await them with excitement. There is an exchange of visions; Peter tells how God spoke to him, and Cornelius shares his own story. Everyone realizes that something special is happening. God is bringing people together! Peter says, "I now realize how true it is that God does not show favoritism but accepts men from every nation who fear him and do what is right" (Acts 10:35). Now that statement may sound obvious to you—a nice truism. It's hard to appreciate what an incredible statement it was at the time. This is a paradigm-shifting moment in the history of Christianity. People are realizing what God has known all along—*he loves everyone.* Yet we still struggle to take in that message today.

It's so difficult to escape our pride and presuppositions, to simply go out and experience people for who they are. I can remember being a guest preacher at a conference. As I was waiting to walk to the platform, I noticed a black lady who was going to be the guest singer. I was looking forward to her singing some soulful gospel music with a little R&B to it. I just made that assumption in my mind because of the color of her skin. Then when she stepped up to sing, what came out was country music, more Nashville than Motown. My own surprise made me realize just how ruled by presumption I am. Like most folks, I have too much of a tendency to force people into cut-and-dried categories with neat labels that I slap onto their foreheads the first moment I meet them.

God is taking us on a journey, as he took Peter on a journey. I imagine that Peter had all kinds of stereotypes shattered in those days he spent with Cornelius. He must have found out that gentiles—a pretty broad category, by the way, because it means "everyone in the world except Jewish people"—don't all walk and talk alike. I bet he discovered they were more like him and his Jewish friends than not. After all, they were all created by the same God.

The Lord has been trying to get us to read that memo for many thousands of years, but we seem to like it our way. We keep classifying people into categories. We have our denominations. We have our political parties, our racial separations, our social classes. We know a thousand ways to divide, but have rarely sought ways to unite. We keep building walls, but Christ wants to disassemble every brick and put it into the construction of a bridge that brings us together in him. Then we can arrive at journey's end and have the amazing experience that Peter had.

The end of the story says that the Holy Spirit descended in an incredible way. The Jews that were there could not deny it: the Holy Spirit didn't care who he blessed, Jew or gentile, man or woman, soldier or civilian. Peter baptized everyone there, and a new day began for the church. When we come together and refuse to allow non-essential differences to divide us, God shows up and the real celebration begins. Then every knee bows, and every tongue confesses that Christ is Lord. The only thing missing is pride.

Isn't it time you break away from the prison of pride and let God take you on a journey?

10.

Get Over Your Small Ambitions: God's Blessings Are Infinite

~

This whole new culture of the Internet makes for some interesting stories, doesn't it? I heard a good one some time ago, and it's true. It's the story of one red paperclip.

That little item, nearly worthless, was just about all Kyle MacDonald had. He had a dead-end career, no money at all, and seemingly few options for an exciting life. Then he came up with a plan that most people would dismiss as ridiculous.

Kyle decided he would get on the Internet and trade his paperclip for something. Then, whatever he could get, he would trade again—trading *up*, hopefully. He would keep on doing this until the cycle ended in exchanging whatever he had for a house.

Go ahead and laugh; aren't all the great ideas laughed at in the beginning? Kyle traded his paperclip for a fish-shaped pen. Not much of a start, right? He traded again, this time swapping the pen for a doorknob. It wasn't the house he wanted, but you could say it was a small part of that house.

Then he managed to trade the doorknob for a Coleman stove, which he soon exchanged for an electric generator.

Next: a Budweiser sign and a keg of beer, which he traded for a snowmobile. Apparently he was becoming adept at what Donald Trump calls the Art of the Deal by this time. The media was interested in the developing story. One year and 14 trades later, Kyle MacDonald exchanged a part in a Hollywood movie for a home in Saskatchewan, Canada.

You could add that he traded his story for a book deal and then a movie deal. It all started with one red paperclip. These events happened between 2005 and 2006—Kyle's bridge from nothing much to something wonderful.

That story makes me think about the miraculous nature of our faith. I think about the incident at the burning bush, when God asked Moses, "What is that in your hand?" It was nothing but an ordinary shepherd's staff in Moses' hand, but in the hand of God, that stick became a serpent that startled the pharaoh and helped lead to the freedom of the children of Israel.

I think about the tiny mustard seed, almost microscopic, that may have rested in the palm of Jesus as he talked about faith. "It takes faith no bigger than this," Jesus said, "to move a mountain." Newton's physical laws would say that's impossible—a mustard seed dislodging a mountain!—but God's eternal law says that *all* things are possible. I can do all things through Christ who strengthens me. You see, the secret is that none of these amazing things are based on the size of whatever lies in your hand. Miracles are based on the power and will of God at work in his obedient servants.

Now, having thought about that, imagine you're standing on a hill just outside Jerusalem. The resurrected Jesus has brought you there, 40 days after the greatest miracle in earth's history. These weeks since the empty tomb have passed like a dream. The Master is giving you a few final thoughts, obviously intending to leave soon. The last words from his mouth are these:

*All authority in heaven and on earth has been given
to me. Therefore go and make disciples of all nations,
baptizing them in the name of the Father and of the
Son and of the Holy Spirit, and teaching them to obey
everything I have commanded you. And surely I am
with you always, to the very end of the age.*
(Matthew 28:18-20)

So shocking is this command that it's easy to miss the
first sentence, which explains the whole thing. Jesus is about
to ascend to heaven, to sit at the right hand of the Father.
Behind him are eleven men, eleven frankly unimpressive
men—let's just come out and admit that.

These men have struggled with just about every chore
Jesus gave them. On one occasion he sent them out to try
their hand at ministry and miracles, and they came back
excited, but puzzled. All the way to Jerusalem, as Jesus had
told them he would face crucifixion, they were arguing about
which of them was the most special. You or I might have
looked at them and observed that at the moment, the answer
was none of the above.

Yet Jesus never fired a single disciple, even that scheming
associate he knew would betray him. He had the most important task in world history to get done, he had an eternity's
worth of teaching and training to accomplish in only three
years, and he stuck with these twelve bumbling fishermen,
tax collectors, zealots, and peasants. This, the unlikely entourage for the one eternal Son of God.

Then, even as these men seemed to have made no prog-
ress over three years—none that we can easily detect from
the gospel stories—he left them with this command. "Oh,
and please: After you've walked back down the hill, keep
on walking until you've been to every corner of this earth.
Share the good news with everyone you can—even though
I won't be physically there to take the lead. Even though

you seem to have learned very little about miracles or my teaching. Even though you are politically powerless in the Roman empire. Even though most of you have no education or money or wisdom.

"You do, of course, have one thing: the promise of the one with all the power and authority of heaven itself."

Ah, yes! That was that preamble to his commission. That part makes a big difference, doesn't it? The secret of our faith and our vision is one thing: we represent the one who has all power and authority. That's how it happened, the triumph of a Christianity which had no worldly power, over the greatest political empire in world history. What else could explain it? I can squint my eyes and project my imagination as far as possible, but to accept eleven ordinary men defying the Roman empire and ultimately spreading their faith to every continent—well, I'm going to need the realm of the supernatural to accept that one.

And if I'm going to experience in my own life all that God wants to do, I'm going to need a little supernatural assistance as well.

Feeling His Pleasure

In this book we've talked about connecting with other people in a more loving way. Our overarching metaphor (no pun intended) is that of a bridge: build it and get over it. We've built little bridges, like the kind that span narrow creeks, to individuals with whom we've struggled to get along. I hope this book has shown you the way toward reconciliation with at least some of the problem relationships in your life.

As we've explored that topic, we've realized we were unlocking a genuine secret to life. The more bridges we built, the greater the network of love for God's kingdom. We find ourselves reconciling with others, loving and being loved more deeply, and finally becoming peacemakers between second and third parties. What a joy it is to live that way. Suddenly life just seems to open up. We're freed from the prison of pride that we discussed in the last chapter. The more lives with which we connect, the richer our own lives are.

And yes, we find ourselves participating in the great work of God during this age. There is the perspective to see the larger bridge that is being built—not over creeks or streams or even rivers, but over the vast, yawning canyon that separates the hurting people of this world from the God who is their only hope. Sometimes that seems impossible—but so was freeing a nation with a wooden stick, or reaching the entire globe with a handful of questionable servants.

What makes the impossible possible is that we have the power and the glory of God behind us. His deepest will is to use us within this world to do great and awesome works for him. Many times in this book I've repeated a favorite verse, "For we are God's workmanship, created in Christ Jesus to do good works, which God prepared in advance for us to do." Yes, in advance. Before you were ever born, God had a plan for your life. Then he intricately designed you to do certain things.

He also designed you to be the most joyful in life when you're doing them, and the least joyful when you are the farthest from doing them. You're like Eric Liddell, the Olympic track star whose story is told in the movie "Chariots of Fire." Liddell said, "I believe God made me for a purpose, but he also made me *fast*. And when I run, I feel His pleasure."

When you do the thing you were created to do, you, too, will feel his pleasure as well as plenty of your own. You'll feel the deepest joy of all when you build bridges between other people and their Creator.

That's the final bridge, the great bridge that Jesus dedicated on that hill before he left this physical earth to join his father. He has countless tasks for us, countless visions to be fulfilled. But every one of them is part of the greater, more comprehensive vision to reconcile the people of earth to their heavenly father. You might own a business. You might sing in a choir. You might run track, like Eric Liddell. You might sweep floors or raise children. Whatever your task, your true purpose is to know God and to make him known to others.

It's a wonderful day when the eyes of your soul come to rest upon that final bridge. When it happens, you'll find God doing three things in your life.

1. Exposure

First, God will give you exposure to new things in life. "Call to me and I will answer you and tell you great and unsearchable things you do not know" (Jeremiah 33:3). That's an exciting thought, isn't it? "Great and unsearchable things" that he has been waiting to show us; waiting until the proper time when we would be ready. Think about Jesus in the Upper Room, the night before he would be crucified. He told them it was better that he go, because the Helper would come. They weren't ready at that moment to experience Pentecost. Peter wasn't ready to have the experience he had in the home of Cornelius, when the Spirit came and there was great love between Jew and gentile. None of them were ready for the miracles they would perform in the book of Acts.

Every generation is like a world of children who have never seen Christmas. God is saying to us, "Oh, the things I can't wait to show you! The sights, the gifts, the music, the celebration." We've been talking about the first days of the church, just after Jesus left. Acts 11 tells how the disciples got the word about Peter in the home of Cornelius.

Can you even imagine how they must have looked at each other and scratched their heads? "Peter? *Our* Peter?" This was the guy who was distraught, inconsolable after Jesus was arrested and crucified. This was the man Jesus had to gently restore at that beach breakfast recounted at the end of John's gospel. Peter had been a mess, frankly. Jesus always loved him, but the disciples knew that he was a mess! And now that same Peter was baptizing homes full of gentiles. He was fearlessly preaching the gospels in the same streets of Jerusalem in which he had three times denied he even knew Jesus.

To you, my friend, God is saying, "I'm going to show you what that's like, this thing that Peter experienced. And everything about your old life will be as different, as much *old history*, as Peter's old life compared to the history of the one who became the lion of the early church.

Once you truly commit yourself to living for God, to building bridges, then you can begin to watch for the things God will show you. It will be exciting; it will be a daily adventure. Have you ever traveled on another continent? Europe, Africa, Asia? Remember the newness, the excitement? That will be your life every day once you become totally, exclusively the property of God's movement in this world. Growth is newness, and you will be growing rapidly.

What you will learn to do is to watch the movements of God. You'll notice him teaching you certain specific lessons. Weeks or months will go by and you'll say, "Here is this one thing God is wanting me to learn right now." And he'll be chipping away at the old you, sculpting you into the new one as he transforms you to the image of his son. God is at work in you to will and to do his good pleasure, as we learn in Philippians. Sometimes life will feel repetitive. You'll keep brushing up against certain attitudes and assumptions you've always had, and then you'll recognize that God is trying to break you out of that. "How long am I going to keep experiencing this?" you'll ask. And you'll hear the still, small voice replying, "Until you learn what I want you to learn.

Until you are prepared to lay this one on the altar of sacrifice, so that you can experience righteousness, peace, and joy."

Michelangelo was the greatest sculptor of the Italian Renaissance. He worked from marble that would come out of quarries, and he cared enough about it that he supervised the mining of it himself. He looked for the best marble that he could get his hands on, but he knew that no stone was perfect. His statues took years to complete (you've probably seen his statue of David, or the one called the *Piéta* that is the crucified body of Jesus on Mary's lap), and he would chip away very slowly at the block of stone, months upon months before you would even recognize what he was sculpting. When he started, it was a great, rectangular block. The final, beautiful art was invisible except to the mind of the artist. Someone asked him the secret to his incredible craft, and he gave the example of sculpting as a subject: one angel. He said, "I start with the stone as it is, and I see in my mind's eye an angel trapped within it. My job is to chip away at everything that is not the angel, until that beautiful creature is liberated from the stone."

We are God's workmanship; he is the sculptor and we are the stone. He sees in us the eternal, perfected creature that is our destiny—the "angel" inside the stone. And he will chip away at everything that is not the angel until we are free. The pick, pick, pick of the chisel can be painful at times, but things that are valuable and worthwhile sometimes require a little pain and sacrifice. The implement in the artist's hand is the sum total of the experiences of your life, and he will expose you to new things, places, and people.

The Holy Spirit is faithful to his task on helping us. So you can expect to hear him whispering in your ear, telling you about the new person you can be. He is all about planting your feet on higher ground. I challenge you to keep watch and see how God begins doing this in your life.

2. Enlightenment

Acts 11 tells the aftermath of Peter's experience in Cornelius' house. He was basically called on the carpet by the other disciples, who are described as "the circumcised believers."

I can imagine them saying, "Bro, have you lost your mind? You intentionally walked into the home of a Roman soldier, an impure gentile, one of our mortal enemies—and you even ate with those people?"

Isn't it interesting that these, the disciples of Jesus, could sound so much like the Pharisees who were always knocking Jesus over the head with cold, unfeeling legalisms? Jesus would give sight to a man blind from birth, and all the teachers would care about was that he did it on the Sabbath. And now, when Peter baptized a large family into the faith, the disciples could only care about sharing a meal with ritually impure gentiles. It's what we might call another adventure in missing the point.

Peter began to speak. He went all the way back to the rooftop and told the story from there—how the voice of God had told him to ignore the ancient dietary laws; how he had obeyed with great reluctance; how he had continued in obedience by traveling with the gentile messengers; and how the Holy Spirit had been so present, and poured out so much joy, in the home of Cornelius.

Don't you imagine that Peter, in telling the story, suddenly realized how far he had come, and the radical enlightenment that now separated him from his closest friends? He was sounding less like his old self and more like the voice with whom he had argued on the rooftop. Peter was explaining how all foods, and all people, are created by God. His discourse may well have reminded the disciples of the last words of Jesus that referred to every corner of the world.

And as he spoke, he must have seen the dubious faces of the unenlightened.

Have you ever made pictures out of the clouds? You might be gazing into the sky on a pleasant day with white, billowy clouds performing their slow, stately dance overhead. Your friend says, "Look, do you see that? It's a picture of Jesus, the way he looked when he walked on the water!"

You look up and ask, "Which cloud? I don't see it."

Your friend offers a few coordinates, and you turn your head around in just the right way until you see what he means. "I see—that's his head over here, and he has his left hand up, right? And he's striding forward."

"Yes! That's it." And the two of you quietly watch the cumulous canvas until its picture has transformed to something else. Once you see that picture, it is very clear; it can't be anything else but the association your mind has established. But you either perceive it or you don't.

I think that's the way Peter found himself when he was answering the disciples' questions. "Can't you see it?" he wanted to ask. "Can't you see Jesus in this picture? Here's the hand of Jesus in this event."

That's what enlightenment is. Once you see the big picture of what God is doing, a certain wisdom comes to you, and you wonder why everyone else can't see the same thing. Once you see Christ performing another miracle, you can't take your eyes off it. And you find yourself looking above all the time, waiting to see what God is going to do next. He is going to be showing you things all the time now that he has your attention. He will do it in your private devotion time, as His Spirit teaches you things in the Bible and through prayer. He will do it through the circumstances around you; you'll understand the world in a whole new way, see it through brand new eyes. And he'll also enlighten you through other believers. Proverbs 27:17 tells us that as iron sharpens iron, one person sharpens another, and be ready—God will send good people to sharpen you.

It has certainly happened in my life that way. I've already mentioned how an original goal of ministry for us was to reach out through the medium of radio. In the early 1990s, we were on the air in the Bay Area at 8:30 on Sunday evenings—one station only. These days Enduring Truth is heard each weekday on stations throughout the country, and we're thankful to God for the fruitfulness of the endeavor. But can you believe it started with me calling a station manager a racist?

Back when we had the one show per week, the Sunday night slot meant a great deal to us. We had a regular group of listeners who would let us know they heard us every weekend at that time.

One day I got a letter from the general manager of the station. He wanted us to know that he was thinking about adding a live, call-in national show to the Sunday evening line up, but this would require him to make some schedule changes. He asked how I'd feel about moving our broad- cast to Saturday evening. As I read the letter, it pushed an emotional button in me that I didn't know I had. I assumed our local, church-sponsored program was being bumped out of a primetime slot to make room for a national ministry with big bucks. I also suspected that as a black pastor, I was seen and being treated as less important than the guy who conducted the call-in show. Money and race.

These thoughts and emotions drove me to reply via email. I wrote this general manager whom I'd never met, I told him I resented being pushed aside for the sake of the syndicated show, and I told him why. Naturally, when he read the email, he was offended. He responded forthrightly to my charges and reminded me that airing my program on their radio station was a privilege I had been afforded as a local pastor rather than a right I was entitled to exercise. He then offered to remain in dialogue with me about the decision he was pondering. As I read his reply, I heard the commentary of the Holy Spirit, whispering in my ear. The still, small voice was saying, *Here's what's going on. You have never met this man, yet you judged him. You made some insulting assumptions about his character and motives, and you're wrong.* I knew it was true and I began to repent in my heart.

But the Spirit wasn't finished speaking. I heard him telling me, *This isn't going to be a quiet repentance kind of thing. You're one of my leaders. I expect more from you, so I want you to go to this man with a letter of apology and straighten things out.* I've dealt with God long enough to know he meant business. There was no point in putting it off. So I drafted the apology letter, drove to the station, and asked for a brief appointment with this man. We spent 90 minutes together. It turned out that he couldn't have been any more the opposite of my presumptions. This man was an experienced and compassionate former pastor with a heart for God. Furthermore, he had a desire to encourage and support local churches like mine. "I don't listen to many of the weekend broadcasts" he said, "but I listen to yours. I'm a fan, and all you had to do was come to me and tell me your concerns. I simply had no idea that the Sunday night slot meant so much to you. I'd have been willing to say no to the national ministry. I wouldn't have done it for just anyone, but I would have done it for you." I felt about three inches tall sitting across from this good man.

Enlightenment can be uncomfortable; so can the sculpting of the Master Artist who is chipping away everything that isn't the angel. It took something like this to teach me about some of the issues that lived inside me. I had to learn in such a way that I would never forget the lesson, and my encounter with a station manager was just what the doctor ordered. The man's name is Ron Walters. Now an executive with national clout in the field of Christian radio, Ron has become one of my most trusted and respected friends. And God used him not only to help me grow as a bridge building Christian, but also to develop into a national broadcaster. On a few occasions when I've spoken at events where he was in attendance, I've humored audiences by saying that Ron and I became friends when I called him a racist!

Great things happen when we build bridges.

3. Endorsement

Have you ever stopped to consider how much time we spend either ignoring or actually resisting God's direction?

The fact is that after God exposes us to new things, and enlightens us with new wisdom, we establish a kind of growth momentum. Life is simply better, because we know we're becoming more like Christ. We find that our relationships with others are blossoming. Our ministry as believers is becoming more fruitful, and our impact is increasing rapidly in a number of directions. We're discovering more significance. The final thing that happens between God and us is *endorsement*. That simply means agreeing with all that the Lord wants to do through us. It sounds simple, but it's incredibly significant because we've previously spent so much of life ignoring or resisting his guidance.

Now we're actually gaining the wisdom to cooperate with God, to endorse his will. That takes special maturity, but it's expected for every one of us. Have you ever taken a child to the doctor to get a shot? If so, you know how children will produce any level of noise, scamper to any corner of the examination room, do anything but let that doctor gently do his work. As the child grows older, he will still put up a little resistance. The time comes eventually when there is enough maturity with the reasonable person, however, to submit to the doctor's ministrations once the patient has been dragged into the office.

A really mature adult actually becomes proactive. He will make appointments with a doctor or dentist when necessary. He may even go to a health club and put his body through all kinds of perspiration and muscle-weariness to stay in good physical shape.

That's normal human endorsement of basic health considerations. In the spiritual world, endorsement means the gradual process of moving from that childishness that fights God's discipline, to the full maturity of the wise believer who understands that the life of simple faith and unquestioning obedience is indeed the best life. This person will do the obvious things: get deep into God's Word, invest himself in church fellowship and ministry, share the gospel with others. But he won't compartmentalize what he has with God, because he will now see Christ everywhere, in every facet of his life. He is grabbing a fellow believer, and saying, "Look! There's Jesus here. And Jesus is at work over there!"

Jesus is no longer a momentary image in the cloud above; the mature believer sees Christ at work in his heart as he stops to talk to that frustrated co-worker at the office. He sees Christ at work as he addresses the need of the neighbor that lives across the street. In fact, he sees his Lord in "the least of these," as Jesus put it. He knows that when he serves the needy, feeds the hungry, helps someone experience freedom in Christ who has been held captive by some vice or besetting sin, he is serving the Son of God. And there's joy to be had in every act of service.

That's the ultimate miracle—our own transformation to the image of Christ himself. It's not really a conscious thing; we're too busy working for the kingdom to even stop much and think about it. But slowly, surely, every day, the previously worldly person is being chipped away, and the image of Christ inside is being liberated in this world.

Can you imagine what this world would be like next year if every community had a man or a woman who was endorsing the work of God in his or her life, so that Christ himself began to walk the streets of that community through one more person? There would be more occasions like the one Peter experienced at Cornelius's house, when the special surprise guest was the Holy Spirit, and everyone forgot all their social, economic, and spiritual barriers and became a family. There would be fewer battles and more parties among us.

If just a few of us got this ball rolling, and let God expose us and enlighten us, so that we endorsed his program, there would be a construction boom in our world—bridges being built everywhere. In this time, when there is so much division, so much name-calling, so many people clustering into little interest groups to shake their fists at all the other interest groups—don't we need to start building a few bridges?

Close your eyes for a few minutes and imagine that world. Imagine the walls coming down, and the bridges extending. We could begin to build those bridges and get over them. And when all of them become one, we could walk across it together to the heavenly city—the place where the Father of us all is eager to gather us up in his arms. We can get over a lot of things, but we'll never get over the joy of that moment.

LaVergne, TN USA
28 September 2009
159271LV00004B/2/P